THE NON-JUDGMENTAL CHRISTIAN

Five Lessons That Will *Revolutionize* Your Relationships

John Kuypers

PRESENT LIVING & LEARNING, INC.
www.presentliving.com

Also by **John Kuypers**

What's Important Now
**Shedding the Past
So You Can Live in the Present**
©2002

FIVE LESSONS THAT WILL REVOLUTIONIZE YOUR RELATIONSHIPS

Lesson 1: YOU SET THEM FREE

"Do not **judge**, or you too will be **judged**. For in the same way you **judge** others, you will be **judged**, and with the measure you use, it will be measured to you." *Matthew 7:1-2 (NIV)*

Lesson 2: YOU ARE REAL, NOT NICE

"Do you bring in a lamp to put it under a bowl or a bed? Instead, don't you put it on a stand? For whatever is hidden is meant to be disclosed, and whatever is concealed is meant to be brought out into the open." *Mark 4:21-22 (NIV)*

Lesson 3: YOU ARE COMPASSIONATE, NOT RIGHTEOUS

"You, therefore have no excuse, you who pass **judgment** on someone else, for at whatever point you **judge** the others, you are condemning yourself, because you who pass **judgment** do the same things." *Romans 2:1 (NIV)*

Lesson 4: YOU ARE WISE, NOT SMART

"First take the **plank** out of your own eye, and then you will see clearly to remove the speck from your brother's eye." *Matthew 7:5 (NIV)*

Lesson 5: YOU ARE PURPOSEFUL, NOT SUCCESSFUL

"As for the person who hears my words but does not keep them, I do not **judge** him. For I did not come to **judge** the world but to save it." *John 12:47 (NIV)*

Published by Present Living & Learning, Inc.
Burlington, ON Canada L7R 3X4
www.presentliving.com

Library and Archives Canada Cataloguing in Publication

Kuypers, John, 1957–
    The non-judgmental Christian : five lessons that will revolutionize your relationships / John
Kuypers.

ISBN 0-9689684-2-2

1. Judgement—Religious aspects—Christianity.   2. Self-help techniques.
I. Title.

BV4501.3.K89 2004   248.4   C2004-905398-1

• Scripture taken from *THE HOLY BIBLE, NEW INTERNATIONAL VERSION*.
  Copyright © 1973, 1978, 1984 by International Bible Society. Used by permission of
  International Bible Society. All rights reserved.
• Excerpts marked NAB are from the *New American Bible with Revised New Testament and
  Psalms* Copyright © 1991, 1986, 1970 Confraternity of Christian Doctrine, Inc., Washington,
  DC. Used with permission. All rights reserved. No portion of the *New American Bible* may
  be reprinted without permission in writing from the copyright holder.

Cover & Text Design/Page Layout: Heidy Lawrance Associates, www.hlacreative.com

Printed in Canada

TABLE OF CONTENTS

FOREWARD

Welcome! I greet you in the name of God our Father, Jesus His precious Son and the Holy Spirit. You are about to read a book that invites you to revolutionize your relationships–with love! Love is what we are all searching for, hoping for and aching for. Love is why we want to please our mom and impress our dad. Love is why we get married and have children. Love is the reason Jesus came to this earth–to show us the Way.

When love is missing, we hurt deeply and profoundly. With nearly one in two marriages ending in divorce, even among Christians, we have learned to abandon each other rather than face the pain. The result is broken trust, simmering anger and fragile hearts. Children grow up in one-parent homes, lifesavings are wiped out and dreams are destroyed. For those who remain committed "till death do us part," many will endure a lifetime of shared loneliness—married in body but divorced in spirit.

Divorce is against Christian teaching. Marriage without love is a spirit-crushing alternative. The Lord has called me, a judgmental man, to speak out on one extraordinary solution: **"Do not judge."** (MT 7:1 NIV) On this foundation, I humbly offer you five lessons that will feed the fire of the love of the Holy Spirit from within yourself.

These lessons are often based on my own real-life experiences because judgments are the intentions that lie buried deeply within a person's heart, and the only heart I have full access to is my own. At times, the detail is personal and revealing, which is needed to illustrate the surgically precise nature of transforming our judgmental, sinful nature. I ask you to respect the fact that the stories that support these five lessons are not about the characters. They are people I love whom God has used to humble me for His glory.

Judgments feed on each other like a cancer. Scripture tells us that it is the Christian man who must take the lead to break this vicious cycle. St. Paul wrote, **"Husbands, love your wives, just as Christ loved the church and gave himself up for her to make her holy."** (EPH 5:25:26 NIV) Paul further describes this as "holy and blameless" in Ephesians 5:27. Blameless means "without judgment." For this reason, the lessons are often written from a man's perspective. If you are a Christian woman and do the same, then surely you will both be blessed with a joyful marriage, centered children and loving relationships throughout your lives!

Let's begin with a timeless prayer of encouragement:

> ### The Prayer of St. Francis of Assisi
> *Lord, make me an instrument of your peace.*
> *Where there is hatred, let me sow love;*
> *Where there is injury, pardon;*
> *Where there is doubt, faith;*
> *Where there is despair, hope;*
> *Where there is darkness, light;*
> *And where there is sadness, joy.*
>
> *O Divine Master,*
> *Grant that I may not so much seek*
> *To be consoled as to console;*
> *To be understood as to understand;*
> *To be loved as to love;*
> *For it is in giving that we receive;*
> *It is in pardoning that we are pardoned;*
> *And it is in dying that we are born to eternal life.*

—John Kuypers
September , 2004

Lesson 1

YOU SET THEM FREE

Judgments cause people to become deaf. Non-judgment opens their ears and their hearts. The effect can be quite dramatic.

I learned this simple truth the hard way. I am a forty seven year old divorced man who is remarried. I left my first wife after a ten year marriage. Two years later, I surrendered my life to Jesus. Our only son Jared was five months old when my wife and I separated. We went to court eight times over the following two years, fighting mostly over child access. She got sole custody. I got generous access. Sole custody means I have no legal rights in the areas of schooling, location, extra-curricular activities, religion, healthcare and principal residence. I lost control of my son when he was just two years old. Accepting this was a bitter pill. I swallowed it though, as fully and completely as I could in the eyes of the Lord. In turn, God has used this reality to teach me how to seek influence instead of control. A wonderful example happened to me, to the benefit of my son, four years later. He was six, and about to begin first grade.

I wanted to send Jared to a French immersion school rather than the regular English school. I had my reasons. I speak French. My second wife is French Canadian. My three stepchildren all attend French immersion schools. Learning a second language is much easier at a young age, and is a gift for life. In our school system, he was required to enter the program in the first grade or not at all, and he would have been allowed to switch back to the mainstream English school at any time.

I suggested the idea to my ex-wife, all too aware that she had final decision-making authority. She didn't like the idea very much. Still, she didn't say no right away. She said she preferred that he went to the neighborhood school. She said he would have more friends living nearby. She also didn't feel comfortable not being able to help him with his French homework, since she didn't speak French herself. I quietly wondered if she felt threatened by this move "closer" to Dad.

1

I invited her to attend the school information night. She declined. I gave her the name of another parent who already had a son in the French immersion school, and was about to send her daughter who had been in Jared's kindergarten class. This mother also spoke no French herself. Two weeks later, she admitted she hadn't called this mother. She simply wasn't interested. She had already made up her mind.

I reluctantly and immediately gave up.

That in itself must have shocked her. The man she was once married to would have persisted, pressuring her with logical facts and arguments, ending with a plea like, "C'mon. What have you got to lose?" Perhaps the old me would have gotten a friend or her parents to speak to her too. Maybe I would have tossed in a couple of digs along the way, just out of frustration. You know, "It's always got to be your way," or "You are so-o stubborn!"

Not this time.

Two months later, the new school year loomed. I called her. I felt totally at peace about Jared missing this once-in-a-lifetime opportunity. I thought, "*I was twelve before I took a single class and I learned the language! If the Lord wants him to speak French, he'll speak French.*" Still, I felt the Spirit prompting me to have one last conversation with her.

The phone call lasted forty-five minutes. I was frank. This was his last chance. "Is it worth a brief chat?" I asked. "Yes," she said. Then I listened, empathized and listened more. I acknowledged the validity of her concerns. I made no effort to "sell" her. She began asking me questions, which I answered as best as I could. Suddenly and without warning, she said, "What the heck, let's give it a try. I can always pull him out if I don't like it."

I nearly fell off my chair. Praise God!

A few moments later, I asked her, "That was a pretty big shift. What made you change your mind?"

She thought for a moment. "To be honest," she said, "I think it was the way you didn't pressure me like you have so often before."

I am not making this up. Honest. She really said that.

In this story, five leadership lessons were in action:

1. **You Set Them Free.** I accepted and supported her freedom to make her own decision. I would have failed before I even began if I felt judgmental about her even having that legal right in the first place. (It's a pre-emptive law in our jurisdiction.)

2. **You Are Real, not Nice.** I spoke my truth from the heart without any criticisms. If I was judgmental in my heart, I would have had to either hide my real thoughts and feelings, or expose my judgmental disapproval, triggering a similar response from her.

3. **You Are Compassionate, not Righteous.** I listened to her actively and with empathy. I could not have done so if I felt judgmental about "flaws" in her thinking or her rejection of my reasoning. I would have jumped in or been defensive.

4. **You Are Wise, not Smart.** I invited her to reconsider her decision. At no time did I pressure her to do it my way. Instead, I acted like a coach, helping her to see all of her choices including how to change her mind if she later preferred.

5. **You Are Purposeful, not Successful.** I persisted in God's will and timing. I could not have done so if I felt paralyzed with unhappy judgments about her decision and about my failure to get what I wanted the first time around.

Judgments cause hardening of the heart. When asked why Moses gave permission to divorce, Jesus said, "It was because your hearts were hard that Moses wrote you this law." (MK 10:5 NIV) Non-judgment softens the heart and opens the ears. When you are non-judgmental, you are letting God participate in the decision. The Lord works miracles when you give Him space to reveal His power and glory. You become His instrument, not His replacement.

The evidence of judgments comes in one word: **Disapproval**. People fear your disapproval of them. You fear the same from them. People also cherish your approval, as do you from them. The desire to gain approval and to avoid disapproval is the judgmental undercurrent in the river of life, constantly dragging you in one direction—blame and shame. To not judge is like leaping out of the river of "this world" and onto the banks of the river. Suddenly, the river becomes clear. Relationships that were foggy, ugly and painful reveal themselves for what they are—a flurry of judgmental pressures by well-intentioned people who are trying to control one another to get what they want. Jesus teaches us that Christians are to go in the opposite direction of this world. "He said to them, 'You belong to what is below, I belong to what is above. You belong to this world, but I do not belong to this world. That is why I told you that you will die in your sins. For if you do not believe that I AM, you will die in your sins.'" (JN 8:23-24 NIV)

Like driving an automobile, you cannot shift in the opposite direction without first passing through neutral. To not judge is to shift into neutral, with your engine still running. You are not in park, shut down and detached from life. You are alive and ready for action! When you shift into neutral about the people pains in your life, you then become capable of shifting gears in the opposite direction. You become capable of swimming against Satan's powerful undercurrents of fear, shame and blame. You will only be able to do so with a deep faith that God is in charge and that there is no need for you to control other people. Not judging others or yourself will dramatically deepen your faith and trust in the Lord.

By itself, non-judgment is an attitude and an intention, built on a foundation of love in your heart. Upon this foundation, you learn how to seek *influence* with your loved ones instead of *control*. This influence comes more readily when you have strong and clear personal boundaries. Throughout this book, you will be asked to examine your relationships by asking yourself, *"Whose space is this?"* If it is their space, your challenge will be to *support* their freedom to do things their way, not your way. If it is your space, your challenge will be to *resist* their attempts to pressure you to do things their way instead of your way. This is the reason for the "Steady Hands" symbol on the front cover of this book. The outstretched right hand symbolizes giving them your *support*. The palm-faced left hand symbolizes *resist*.

The alternative to support is *pressure*. I call this "the Hammer." The Hammer uses judgments to force others to change. Broken trust and damaged relationships are the price tags of acting with judgment in your heart. The alternative to resist is to *cave in*. I call this "the Doormat." This is the Hammer in suppressed mode. Resentment is the evidence that you are suppressing a judgment towards someone. Emotional distance and a lack of intimacy are the price tags of being a Doormat with the ones you love. This is a picture of what it looks like to shift from condemnation to non-judgment:

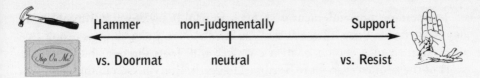

Hammer   non-judgmentally   Support

vs. Doormat   neutral   vs. Resist

The Hammer and the Doormat create a relationship dilemma. If you get sufficiently frustrated with someone, you pull out the Hammer to pressure him or her to change. If the person becomes sufficiently upset with you in return, he or she will counter-attack or abandon you. Fear of this possibility will encourage you to switch to being a Doormat, resentfully putting up with the person's behavior.

If you feel stuck in any relationship, whether it is your spouse, your children, friends or family, the hammer and the doormat will be the evidence that you are caught in this unhappy relationship dilemma. You may even feel stuck within yourself, unhappy with choices you have made and the situations God has thrown your way. The way out each and every time is to first become non-judgmental— before you act. Indeed, you must stop trying so hard and go with the flow of life. When you set others free, you set yourself free.

1-1 The Mind of Christ

Jesus taught non-judgment with his words. "Do not judge or you will be judged." (MT 7:1 NIV) This is not a command. It is a teaching. We are free to judge but we are warned that there will be consequences for doing so. "For in the same way you judge others, you will be judged, and with the measure you use, it will be measured to you." (MT 7:2 NIV) The choice is ours. We can judge but our judgments will boomerang right back at us. For this reason, deciding to be more non-judgmental is in a certain way *selfish* because we are the ones who get to enjoy the biggest rewards! Jesus emphasized the truth of this principle with these words: "I tell you, on the day of judgment people will render an account for every careless word they speak. By your words you will be acquitted, and by your words you will be condemned." (MT 12:36-37 NAB) You are the architect of your own fate. When you are non-judgmental, words rooted in love will come out of your mouth. This is how you will win with the ones you love.

Jesus taught non-judgment with his actions. "If any of you is without sin, let him be the first to throw a stone at her." (JN 8:7 NIV) Non-judgment sets people free to make their own choices of their own free will. Jesus shows us how with the story of the adulteress about to be stoned to death. Every person in that story was set free by Jesus to throw their stones at her, or to set them down. Out of their own free will, not one person threw a stone. Jesus does not "make" us do anything his way, so neither should we in our dealing with others. This is how you can lead others in a way that earns their respect and love. When you are non-judgmental, you dramatically increase your ability to influence people to change, freely and willingly. You increase your impact because you are influencing with love and compassion, not fear and control.

Jesus provided himself a disclaimer on being judgmental. He said, "You judge by appearances, but I do not judge anyone. And even if I should judge, my judgment is valid because I am not alone, but it is I and the Father who sent me." (JN 8:15-16 NAB) This gives Jesus alone the authority to pass judgment on others, for example, when he called the scribes and Pharisees a "brood of vipers," "serpents" and "hypocrites."

James tells us that God alone has the right to judge, and not us. "Brothers, do not slander one another. Anyone who speaks against his brother or judges him speaks against the law and judges it. When you judge the law, you are not keeping it, but sitting in judgment on it. There is only one Lawgiver and Judge, the one who is able to save and destroy. But you—who are you to judge your neighbor?" (JAS 4:11-12 NIV) God has the right to judge and we do not. Nevertheless, the Bible offers us escape clauses. For example Paul, who often writes about non-judgment, also tells us, "What business is it of mine to judge those outside the church? Are you not to judge those inside? Expel the wicked man from among you." (1 COR 5:12-13 NIV) Paul is referring specifically to consequences for believers who engage in sexual immorality, greed, idolatry, slander, drunkenness or dishonesty. Clearly, we are not to judge unbelievers. However, we may judge believers who are guilty of certain sins by severing our relationship with them. But, we know from Jesus' parable of the Prodigal Son that this is not forever. If they repent, we are to forgive them, no matter what. To those who would justify their judgments of other believers on this basis, I pose this question: *"Does it work?"* Does judging other people get them to change in the way you want? And if so, at what price?

Estranged relationships? Anger and resentment? Rebelliousness? People will respond more receptively to you if you first get yourself into a non-judgmental frame of mind, before you speak or act. In this way, your words, tone and manner will radiate compassion and understanding, even if you decide to impose an unpleasant consequence. This will happen for you when you decide to set them free from your approval or disapproval.

Non-judgment at all times is not humanly possible. You must understand and accept this or you risk becoming judgmental about how often you fail to be non-judgmental! Learning not to judge is a life-long journey. If you are judgmental a hundred times a day, your goal is to reduce this to ninety-five, then ninety and so on. Today you overcome one judgment, tomorrow another. Sometimes, it takes months of intentional effort to overcome a judgmental desire to punish someone or to pressure him or her to do things our way. Non-judgment is not linear. We think we get it. Then we discover new layers of judgments within us, a new hardness in our heart that remains to be healed by the Holy Spirit. We are a work in progress.

Non-judgment will increase your dependence on God in your daily life. This is because once you are aware of your judgmental nature, you will notice it…often! Its evidence is inescapably in front of us with every annoying frustration, and every soaring, ego-driven ecstasy. It is like buying a new car and suddenly noticing the same model driven by others. They were there all along— you just didn't notice! For this reason, non-judgment easily becomes a twenty-four hour a day, seven days a week job. With all this evidence flying in your face, you learn to accept your faults. Eventually, non-judgment leads you to be centered, calm and clear in the face of any crisis, free from highs and lows, and filled with self-acceptance in the joy and peace of knowing that God is in control. You accept that the present moment is exactly as it was meant to be. Your only question for God is, *"What is your will for me now, Lord?"*

Non-judgment will invite miracles into your life. I have experienced this joy many times, in my twice-recovered second marriage, my renewed cooperation with my ex-wife, my ability to parent my child through difficult times and even in healing my body from previously unexplained aches and pains. When you focus *first* on being non-judgmental in any difficult, frustrating, anxiety-filled situation, you create for yourself *the mind of Christ*. You are coming from a place of love and peace, not blame, fault-finding and condemnation. You unlock the gift of the Holy Spirit to touch the hearts and souls of those around you. This only happens when you first become non-judgmental in a given situation. This involves giving up control. You will feel this as suffering. You hurt, you rage, you grieve, you feel pain. Until you succeed, Jesus' teaching remains true—your judgments come back to you in the measure you use. When you succeed, you surrender control of the situation to God. Then miracles become possible, and even likely.

Non-judgment is a pre-requisite for effective leadership. When you ask someone to do something, you are being a leader. You are leading the person in the hope that he or she will follow you. If the person does, you have succeeded. If he or she doesn't, you have failed. When you feel no blame or condemnation towards the person for his or her behavior, you will increase your ability to succeed. You will also be at peace if you fail. You will accept that changing other people is not within your control. Jesus never *forced* anyone to follow Him. His disciples followed him freely and willingly. If you are a committed Christian, you are living proof: you follow Jesus freely and willingly.

With a blamefree, loving frame of mind that sets the ones you love free, you become capable of progressing into action mode. These are described in this book as four more lessons that will encourage people to trust you and follow your lead. These additional four lessons are:

Lesson 2: You are real, not nice. (personal integrity)
Lesson 3: You are compassionate, not righteous. (communication)
Lesson 4: You are wise, not smart. (performance-building)
Lesson 5: You are purposeful, not successful. (vision)

Each of these four lessons is demonstrated in the life of Jesus.

Jesus led by being real, not nice. Jesus openly called the high priests "hypocrites." He performed miracles on the Sabbath, in contravention to Jewish law. He drove the sellers out of the temple, without hesitation. While we might call some of his other actions "nice," his motives were always real. As a Christian, being real is how you let your light shine and live as the salt of the earth. Unlike Jesus however, your realness will reveal your judgmental, sinful heart. Revealing this is crucial in order for you to transform your heart. Otherwise, you will suppress the real you, hiding your truth from yourself because of your desire to hide it from those around you. Your private self must become the same as your public self. You must learn to live as if you have *nothing to hide*. Hiding who you are is anchored in judgments about self and others. Hiding inevitably leads to hypocrisy, speaking untruths and exaggerations. Others can see this and you will lose the respect of those you wish to lead. You must seek to be truthful above all else, because "The truth will set you free." (JN 8:32 NIV) On this basis, you will impact others by your humble acceptance of your imperfectness, saved only by His grace and not by your works.

Jesus led by being compassionate, not righteous. Though he is righteous and without sin, Jesus did not use righteousness to condemn those who did not follow him. He used compassion, which means to "suffer with." He prayed while on the cross,"Forgive them, Father for they do not know what they are doing." (LK 23:34 NIV) He did not try to argue with his accusers or to defend himself. He turned the other cheek in humility. Compassion is the ability to see the world through the eyes of other people, even while you yourself are suffering at their hands, innocent of the judgments being made against you. You must learn to live as if you have *nothing to prove*. With nothing to prove, you set aside your desire to use righteousness as the basis for judging others or yourself. Instead, you will open your heart to feel compassionate towards the sins and mistakes of those around you. Your humble compassion will help them to see their own faults and weaknesses out of their own free will, just as Jesus' suffering and death helps us see our sinful nature and accept that we are saved in spite of our unworthiness.

Jesus led by being wise, not smart. Jesus did not attempt to control the behavior of others. A smart man or woman has plenty of answers and uses them to pressure others to do things in his or her "smart" way. Jesus revealed truths and let people freely and willingly change or not, as they saw fit. He advised the rich man in Luke Chapter 18 that if he wanted to inherit eternal life, he needed to give away all of his money and follow Jesus. The rich man sadly declined to follow. Jesus made no attempt to force him or anyone else to follow his teachings. He revealed truth through his words and actions, and people followed him or not, as they pleased. "He who has ears, let him hear." (MT 13:43 NIV) As a follower of Jesus, you must learn to live as if you have *nothing to lose*. When their behavior is not about you, your mind becomes open to see ways in which to intentionally and helpfully influence those you love to change in a non-pressuring way, even as you accept that you cannot force them to change. Such wisdom is above "intelligence."

Jesus led by being purposeful, not successful. Jesus knew his Godly purpose and fulfilled it. By man's measure, at the time he was not successful. Peter revealed man's definition of success when he reacted to Jesus' announcement that he would be killed and raised on the third day: "Never, Lord!" he said. "This shall never happen to you! Jesus turned to him and said, "Get behind me Satan! You are a stumbling block to me. You do not have in mind the things of God but the things of men." (MT 16:22-23 NIV) Peter was trying to play God himself. As a Godly believer, you must become skilled at staying true to God's purpose for your life, even when those close to you want you to put earthly success and their own needs ahead of God's will. You must learn to live so that your purpose in life is unmistakably the same as that of Jesus: to **love** God with all your heart, soul and mind, and to **love** your neighbor as yourself. (Mt 22:37-39). Spiritual love will gush forth from within yourself when you live as if you have *nothing to hide, nothing to prove, and nothing to lose*. Then your ability to discern God's will for you will grow immensely because you will be in a state of spiritual surrender. The leadership challenge to be purposeful will often reveal itself around money, values and lifestyle conflicts between you and your spouse.

On a foundation of non-judgment, you transform your character and self-image from being Nice, Righteous, Smart and Successful to one built on being Real, Compassionate, Wise and Purposeful. You will help the people you care about make real changes in their lives that will encourage them to achieve their fullest potential. *Maybe* they will thank you along the way. I say *maybe* because your goal as a leader is for them to change of their own free will. In other words, changing will be *their* idea, not yours. This will only happen if it is true—that changing really *is* their idea, and that you have no prejudiced stake in whether they change or not. You will achieve this when you surrender control over them to God. Indeed, non-judgmental leadership is anchored in the basic premise that God is changing them, not you. For that reason, there is no reason for you to think you did it, though you will allow yourself to be God's instrument in their lives.

Group Study: Set Them Free Lesson 1-1. Was Jesus non-judgmental? Open the gospel. Read any story or parable. As a starter, turn to Matthew 20:1-16. Was the vineyard owner being judgmental when he paid all the vineyard workers the same, though each had worked very different hours? Was Jesus being judgmental when he cast the moneychangers out of the temple in John 2:14-16? What about how Jesus handled the crowd about to stone the adulteress in John 8:3-11?

NOTES

_____

_____

_____

_____

_____

1-2 What is "non-judgmental"?

There is a line between being judgmental and discernment, assessment, and preferences. This book seeks to define that line. We make judgments throughout our daily lives. Not judging is often misconstrued as meaning rolling over and becoming a doormat. However, non-judgment has the opposite effect. Rather than being a pushover, we become more like Jesus himself, who said, "As for the person who hears my words but does not keep them, I do not judge him. For I did not come to judge the world, but to save it." (JN 12:47 NIV) With non-judgment, we become more capable of saving those we care about because we begin to understand and live the true meaning of love. To love is to relentlessly and increasingly die to self by shrinking the ego. Dying to self is the price of being non-judgmental. We can only do so if we rely ever more heavily on Jesus to meet our needs, without "needing" other people, especially our spouse and children, to meet our emotional and spiritual needs. When we need *nothing* from them, we learn how to love them in a spiritual way that earns respect and wins with love.

In its simplest form, non-judgment is acceptance. You are accepting the freedom of others and yourself to be who you are without blame or condemnation. It is like no-fault car insurance. The damage is real. Sin has occurred. Someone has to pay. But no one is at fault. Instead, you focus on *what's important now?* What is the wise response in light of how she feels, what he said, or what a loved has done?

To not judge is to hold a loving, compassionate attitude that does not condemn. Jesus does not condemn us for our sins. Neither are we to condemn others or even ourselves. We are to love our neighbor as we love ourselves. (Mt 22:39) As you do so, you will experience love. I don't mean messy, clingy, co-dependent, romantic love that leans on other people for you to feel fulfilled. I mean spiritual love that leans on God.

I work with many people who are struggling with their marriages or their divorces. Ultimately, every person explains the reason for their unhappiness in this way: "I just don't feel accepted by my partner." This is the evidence that they feel judged by their loved one. When a person feels accepted exactly as they are, he or she feels affirmed and validated as worthy of being loved.

Judgment is the intention that lies secretly in your heart. It is the desire to blame, convict and condemn. The end purpose of judging is to *pressure* other people to change so that we'll feel better, safer and happier. Often it works. Judgments cause other people to react. They almost always work on a child, whose boundaries and assertive skills are too weak to withstand a well-placed judgmental comment or threatening command. When you were a child, judgments molded you. Today as an adult, you must unlearn those judgments. You will most easily recognize them by the terms "trigger" and "button." When people push your buttons, they are triggering your judgments. You, in turn, are doing the same to them.

A person can *speak* the same sentence with the same words in a way that is either judgmental or non-judgmental. "That is fornication," when stated evenly and calmly is a non-judgmental statement of fact. "That is *fornication!*" can be a knife-like accusation that will send chills down the spine of the accused. A person can take the same *action* in a judgmental or non-judgmental way. A young man, still studying in post-secondary education, informs his parents that he has decided to move in with a woman and her child. The father responds by ceasing to provide his son with money that he previously gave to support him, saying, "If you want to be a man in this way, then you must now act like a man who has a family to support." His actions will be judgmental only if his intention is to punish his son and pressure him to leave this woman and return to doing things "Dad's" way. If the father searches his heart and is at peace with his son's freedom to make his own choices, even if he disagrees with them, then cutting him off financially is not judgmental. He is merely exercising his right to do with his money as he pleases. Jesus taught this principle in the parable of the vineyard workers who were paid the same amount for working different lengths of time (Mt 20:1-16). It is the intention in your heart that defines the state of being "non-judgmental."

We judge because judging gives us the temporary sense that we are in control. To not judge is to feel out of control and even irresponsible. We feel that we are *approving* actions with which we disagree. This is false. Not judging is not the same as approving. We are only accepting the other person's *freedom* to say and do what he or she wants. For example, if a friend begins avoiding you and not reciprocating your efforts to contact him, what thoughts run through your mind? What feelings run through your heart? Do you assume the best or the worst? Do you have thoughts of retribution about the next time he needs you and how you will treat him just as disrespectfully? Suppose you were really counting on this person? What can you do? Keep calling? Send him a letter? What will you write? "Please, pretty please call me?" In reality, he is free to break his promise to you, as hurtful and sinful as that may be.

In its highest form, not judging is the ultimate act of forgiveness. You are forgiving your loved one and she doesn't even think she has done anything wrong. When you are non-judgmental, other people are *already* forgiven for hurting you, even as they are doing it! This is what Jesus did with his executors as they hung him on the cross. **"Father, forgive them, for they do not know what they are doing."** (LK 23:34 NIV) This is what will let you be on the receiving end of angry, manipulative, unkind behaviors from others and still feel at peace, aware that their words and actions are not about you. This is the hope and the vision for being non-judgmental.

The reality is often a different story. Personally, I have at times required months of intentional effort to become non-judgmental about someone's behavior. Each time

I do, the effect is cumulative. The judgment "topic" is gone forever, and not only with that person. Whether I felt bothered by his or her dishonesty, hypocrisy or rejection, my eyes were opened and I saw new ways in which to respond to that person in a way that gave me His peace. Such is the impact of non-judgment. You give love and you feel loved in return, though not necessarily from the person you are loving. Your sense of love is coming from Jesus through the grace of the Holy Spirit.

Many people, upon hearing me speak on this topic, respond by saying that if they didn't judge, they would be doormats who let people get away with anything they want. One man said to me with great indignation, "What if a man broke into my house and began raping my wife and daughter? What would have you me do? Stand around and watch?" I said, "Not at all." Before I could go on, the anger rose in his voice and he said, "I would take my fists and beat that man to a pulp, that's what I would do!"

Anyone can understand that kind of reaction. It is a judgmental reaction designed to do the one thing that all judgments seek to do: take control. To accept the possibility that this criminal who has entered your house with evil intent could somehow be a good thing seems inconceivable. Yet being non-judgmental does not result in being a doormat. Being non-judgmental results in being calm, clear and wise in your response so that you actually get what you want, rather than continuing the satanic cycle of hate breeding hate. Non-judgment breaks the cycle of "an eye for an eye," that oft-misquoted phrase from Exodus 21:22.

Control is anchored in fear which comes from Satan. Surrender is anchored in love which comes from God. When God created man, he did so without giving us knowledge of good and evil. Satan's successful temptation of Eve to eat the fruit from the tree in the Garden of Eden was anchored in a judgment by Eve—that what God had given her wasn't good enough. She wanted more. She wanted to be like God Himself! Adam stood by like a doormat and followed her lead. From that moment on, mankind has sought to be like God, just like Satan seeks to be like God. Our desire to judge others is the proof of our inborn sinful nature. The shame that Adam and Eve felt after their sin is further evidence of judgment–self-judgment! They knew they were no longer pure. They were no longer good enough to be in God's presence. Not feeling you are "good enough" is the underlying cause of wanting to be judgmental. Judgment is anchored in pride. Pride comes from the ego. Shrinking the ego leads to humility. Humility is the cornerstone of being non-judgmental.

Judging people and situations gives us the temporary illusion that we *are* better than good enough! When we judge, we are playing God in a way that feeds our ego. We are pronouncing "good" and "bad", "right" and "wrong." The apostle James captures in words our sinful nature when we judge in this way: "For if a man with gold rings on his fingers and in fine clothes comes into your assembly, and a poor person in shabby clothes also comes in, and you pay attention to the one wearing the fine clothes and say, 'Sit here, please,' while you say to the poor one, 'Stand there,' or 'Sit at my feet,' have you not made distinctions among yourselves and become judges with evil designs?" (JA 2:2-4 NAB)

A judgment with an evil design comes about when we compare a person to our pre-conceived beliefs about what is right or wrong, and *then condemn that person.* It is not a judgment to say, "I prefer coffee over tea." Neither is it a judgment to say, "I prefer to spend time with Bob over Bill," or "Barb is better suited for this job than Sue." These are preferences and assessments. Judgments are the attitude behind our words that blame and condemn. Even if we know that a person's behavior is wrong, to judge him or her is to blame them. "Bad boy, Jake!" is a judgmental statement. "That guy is so lazy!" is a statement that condemns. "When are you going to learn how to operate this machine *the right way?*" is a humiliating statement designed to shame a person into performing "better." "This rotten traffic is driving me nuts!" is blaming the traffic for how you feel. "I am so stupid! When will I learn to stop screwing up?" is a condemnation directed towards oneself, which is every bit as unloving and sinful as judging someone else. At a deeper level, the inability to face intimate, emotional moments is anchored in judgments too. We unconsciously sense the moment is "unsafe" and we respond by either withdrawing or by attacking the source by saying something like, "Don't give me that touchy-feely stuff!"

Accepting your desire to be judgmental is a bit like going through the four stages of grieving the loss of a loved one. You will **deny** it, blindly looking away. Then you will feel **angry** about it, justifying it by blaming others for "making" you say and do judgmental acts. Then you will **explore** it to see what happens when you intentionally stop judging a person or situation that bothers you. Finally, you will **accept** it, knowing that you are loved by the Lord in spite of your weakness. You are a judgmental sinner. So am I. You will find this humbling, as I do.

As you stop judging, you will experience the wisdom expressed in Psalm 46:10, "Be still and know that I am God." (NIV) Without judgments, your racing mind will slow down to a fraction of its former speed. You will find yourself in a good mood quite often! You will carry an attitude of gratitude, free from the expectations and limiting beliefs that used to compromise your peace. You are not in control. God is in control! They didn't do it to you. They're just being who they are! You are only in control of how you respond—whether with love and compassion, or fear and control.

You will also notice that the way your mind thinks will change. Paul tells us, "Do not conform any longer to the pattern of this world, but be transformed by the renewing of your mind." (RO 12:2 NIV) When you begin to notice how your mind thinks, you will see that judgments are the primary driver of your thoughts. When we judge or feel judged, we dwell on justifying ourselves. We think, "Sure she's mad at me, but how could I help it? She just barged in and took over. I had to do something!" Judgments cause us to *replay the past.* We want to justify ourselves because we are worried that others will be mad at us. Our mind spins in a frenzy, re-affirming to ourselves that we didn't mess up, that we are good enough and that our unhappiness is another person's fault. If our self-justification fails us, we blame ourselves, experiencing the horrible sinking feeling of shame deep in the pit of our stomach.

These past-oriented thoughts always lead to future-oriented thoughts in which we *role-play the future.* The evidence of this is that you are mentally analyzing and rehearsing what you will say when you meet up with someone whose approval matters to you. Over-analyzing and rehearsing are ways of trying to control what you will say or do in advance of facing your wife, husband, father, mother or difficult teenager. We do this to minimize the chance that we will reveal our judgments of them (for example, by saying the "wrong" thing). We are anxiously hoping to minimize their judgments of us in return! If we don't like how these future scenarios play out in our minds, we tend to avoid the person instead. This is how judgments cause emotional distance and rob us of intimacy in relationships. The love is gone, replaced with judgmental walls.

To judge is to make a comparison. You are comparing what is happening with a past experience or a future expectation. When you don't judge, you are aware of this difference, but you accept it. As a result, you have much less to think about. Your thoughts will be grounded in the present moment, which means that they will be focused on what is happening *now.* You accept that the past is unchangeable. You take ownership of your past with a humble heart, whether you were a superstar or a super-jerk! You trust that God is in control of your future and that fretting about it will only cause your fears to actually come true. When you are present moment-oriented, your mind, heart, body and soul focus on now. You will feel His peace. You are safe in His presence.

God is eternal and so is the present moment. God describes Himself in present moment terms: "God said to Moses, 'I AM WHO I AM. This is what you are to say to the Israelites: I AM has sent me to you.'" (EX 3:14 NIV) The present moment is the definition of eternity. It has never *not* been the present moment. This isn't scriptural or unscriptural—it is merely a logical fact. The more you let go of your judgments, the more you will focus on the present moment where God Himself dwells. Jesus said, "For where two or three are gathered together in my name, there am I in the midst of them." (MT 18:20 NAB) He is present with you right now if you can simply be still, free from your judgmental past and future-oriented thoughts. Then you will hear His voice, feel His love and know His will for you.

Your greatest risk is that you will start to judge all the judgments of others, which you will now notice like a hawk hovering over a field of mice. Beware! This can make you even *more* judgmental than when you were traveling in blissful ignorance. Paul said, "Be kind and compassionate to one another, forgiving each other, just as in Christ God forgave you." (EPH 4:32 NIV) With love in your heart, you will find yourself able to execute the often simple, common-sense techniques offered in this book to deal with people and situations that bother you. When you focus on first being non-judgmental before speaking or acting in a given situation, you will create for yourself the mind of Christ. Paul exhorts, "Live a life of love, just as Christ loved us," (EPH 5:2 NIV)

Here is how I have made sense of what each of us must do to live a life focused on love: **When you have *nothing* but love, you have everything.**

St. Paul captures the truth of this within his famous description of love in 1 Corinthians, Chapter 13:1-4, often quoted at weddings. "If I speak in human and angelic tongues but do not have love, I am a resounding gong or a clashing cymbal. And if I have the gift of prophecy and comprehend all mysteries and all knowledge; if I have all faith so as to move mountains but do not have love, I am **nothing**. If I give away everything I own, and if I hand my body over so that I may boast but do not have love,

I gain **nothing.**" Paul continues in verse 8: "Love never fails. If there are prophecies, they will be brought to **nothing**; if tongues, they will cease; if knowledge, it will be brought to **nothing.**" (NAB)

Paul tells us, if you have *everything* but love, you have nothing. Is it therefore fair to say that if you have *nothing* but love, you have everything? This has been my experience. Paul said, "If anyone thinks he is something when he is **nothing**, he deceives himself." GAL 6:3 (NIV) In order to become a non-judgmental Christian who leaves "loveprints" on your loved ones and on those you touch in life, your goal is to need *nothing* and depend entirely on God. You must live as if you have *nothing to hide, nothing to prove, and nothing to lose.* When you free yourself from your fears that someone will find out something about you, show that you were wrong or cause you to lose something that matters to you, your ability to be non-judgmental will soar.

Group Study: Set Them Free Lesson 1-2. Experience the impact of an intentional attitude. Do this exercise in pairs. Think of a relationship situation that bothers you. Describe your experience to an uninvolved, unbiased partner. Focus on having an attitude of "being passionate," letting out your full emotions. Stop after three-five minutes. Then re-state the same story focused on having an attitude of "being detached," in a clinical, "just-the-facts" way. Finally, re-state your story one more time, focusing on an attitude of "be grateful." Tell the story as if it were the best thing that ever happened to you. As a group, discuss what differences you noted as you looked at the same experience through three different "attitudinal" lenses. Which attitudes shift gears from judgmental to neutral to non-judgmental? How does that feel?

NOTES

Lesson 2

YOU ARE REAL, NOT NICE

A man came to see me, anxiously admitting that he was on the verge of divorce. He was visibly scared. His wife had told him the previous night, "If you don't support me, this marriage is over!" His wife and daughter had had a major fight. He had stood by while his teenage daughter cursed her mother openly and abusively. As he described the background of his marriage, he acknowledged that whenever his wife grew angry, he became "nice." He would make an extra effort to clean up the house, make a fine dinner, and behave in a squeaky clean manner. He gave me a wry grin at one point and said, "No one can accuse me of not being a nice guy."

Being nice can bring your marriage crashing down faster than a barrel over Niagara Falls, if your niceness is not real. In my first marriage, I spent ten years being nice. I twisted myself into a pretzel in a vain attempt to be what I thought she expected me to be—a faithful husband with a good career, who was financially sound and emotionally even-keeled. In reality, I misled her. I suppressed my real feelings and real desires. I was unhappy about major issues in our marriage such as where we lived, having children, sexuality, and relationships with my family. I felt resentful that I was living her life, not mine. My niceness was a lie that created a false sense of security for her. It also created an emptiness within me that gnawed incessantly. I felt a growing certainty that I would die if I did not do something about it. One day, I brought down our marital house of cards in a reckless desire to find myself. I wanted to be real. My goal was a good one. My method was shameful and destructive.

The purpose of this chapter is to give you practical, biblical tools for being real in a loving, respectful way, not in a rebellious, damn-the-torpedoes way. Being real means revealing what you *really* think and feel. Your private self must become the same as your public self. Then you will become integrated and whole. Being real requires mastering the skill of *integrity*. Your mind, body, heart and soul become unified, not splintered by thoughts that think one thing and actions that reflect another.

A recent email joke that reveals what it is to be real crossed my desk recently. A man and woman were traveling separately by train on a long journey. By happenstance, they were booked into the same sleeping cabin. A few minutes after crawling into the upper bunk, the man said to the woman, "I'm feeling a bit cold. Would you mind getting up and passing me the extra blanket over there?"

She replied, "I have a better idea. Would you mind if we considered ourselves married, just for this one night?"

The man's voice brightened up eagerly. "Sure!"

"Great!" she said. "Then get your own darn blanket!"

To which he responded with a loud fart!

To be real is to live as if you have *nothing to hide*. In describing the secret to the kingdom of God, Jesus said, "Do you bring in a lamp to put it under a bowl or a bed? Instead, don't you put it on a stand? For whatever is hidden is meant to be disclosed, and whatever is concealed is meant to be brought out into the open" (MK 4:21-22 NIV) Openness sheds light on darkness. Hiding conceals the darkness of our judgmental nature, which is anchored in shame and pride. Shame and pride are the opposite sides of the same coin. Non-judgment melts that coin, replacing it with humility. When we find fault, we are blaming. When we decide, "Someone is responsible and must pay," we are being judgmental. We do this to hide our shame by papering it over with our pride. Someone has to be a fault, and if it isn't you, it must be me. The ego desperately wants to deny self-blame, resulting in creating a false self…a "nice" self. The effect of denial is to become highly self-absorbed, constantly evaluating whether we are good enough or not.

One way you will know if you are hiding is if you like to avoid conflict. We avoid conflict because of judgments. Blame triggers our shame. We instantly want to defend ourselves, and so we blame other people. We think their unhappiness or critical nature is about us. We are caught in a web of ego-based lies that wants to find fault. The original conflict quickly gets lost in a sea of accusations, threats and retaliatory consequences. We hammer each other, and then we become doormats to avoid the hammer. Non-judgment breaks this deadly relationship-buster. Without a desire to blame or a fear of *being* blamed, you will trust yourself to be frank and open about difficult issues right when they are happening.

But there is a catch to this promised land. You must allow your judgments to *emerge* in order to rid yourself of them. You must allow the shallow, mean, selfish and hypocritical part of you to become visible. When you do, people will be judgmental about you—I guarantee it! That's the bad news. The good news is that your *own* blindness to them will also be lifted. You cannot deny what you have caught yourself saying and doing. In this way, the truth will set you free, just as Jesus promised (John 8:32).

Once you see the real you, you have the great advantage that no unbeliever has—you can fall on your knees and repent, knowing you are loved by Jesus in spite of your sinful nature. Each repentance will heal one more of your judgments. Day by day, month by month, year by year, the Lord will transform your heart in this way. As He does, you will become more and more comfortable in your own skin about who you are. You will be salt and light to others, free from judgmental, punitive intentions in your heart towards others.

I compare this transformation to morphing from a watermelon into a peach. A watermelon is hard on the outside, mush on the inside and takes up a lot of space. A peach is soft on the outside, tough on the inside and takes up very little space. Most of us are like a watermelon. Our judgments are hard walls to keep other people from seeing the soft vulnerable person that lies within. Jesus called this "hardened hearts." We want to control what other people do, what other people think of us, and what kind of life God is supposed to give us. The evidence is our anger and our pain. We want to be in control of space that isn't ours to control.

To not judge is to be like a peach. We shrink our space by giving up controlling others. Instead, we focus on controlling ourselves. We set others free to be who they are. The evidence is that we no longer feel hurt and upset by a myriad of things other people say and do. We can only do this if we are solidly anchored in who we are ourselves…and who we are not.

Jesus as a man was like a peach. He was compassionate towards others, and He had an iron-will to do His Father's will, no matter what the consequences. When we have compassion towards others while being true to God's will for our own lives, we become a force of influence, not of power and control. Princess Diana learned an aspect of this late in her abbreviated life, when she said, "It is none of my business what other people think of me." She humbly accepted her powerlessness to control the thoughts and opinions of others.

Being real will result in many self-revelations, some of which will be small and some which may be huge. In my first marriage, my wife wanted me to put the dirty dishes away right after we finished eating. I stubbornly refused to do so, claiming my right to "do the dishes my way, not your way." A few months after we separated and I was living alone, I noticed a peculiar habit of mine—I was putting the dirty dishes away right after I was done eating! I suddenly realized that for ten years, I had stubbornly and egotistically refused to do what she wanted in order to defiantly do it "my way." My way wasn't real, it was fake! I was being reactive to what I perceived as her criticism of my way of doing the dishes. But I didn't know that until I was alone. Then I saw the real me in action.

All Christians face this same grave danger of being false. The wisdom in the Bible can become a "rule book," teaching us what good behavior looks and sounds like. We "do" the right behavior, but in our hearts, we may not be real. In those moments, we have become like the Pharisees and Sadducees of Jesus' time. We have become legalistic, trying to "earn" the approval of others through our good works. Basic Christian Bible study teaches us that we enter heaven by grace, not by works. Paul writes, **"For by grace you have been saved through faith, and this is not from you; it is the gift of God; it is not from works, so no one may boast."** (EPH 2:8-9 NIV)

Nice works that are not real lead to hypocrisy. We risk being the "good" Christian on Sunday morning who, when he tries to leave the crowded church parking lot, silently feels annoyed with the traffic! Let's not even talk about how he responds when his wife nags him, the kids get on his nerves or a co-worker messes up at work on Monday morning. Of course, others readily see this hypocrisy, though few ever say anything.

As you become more aware of what judgments look like and sound like, you will see that they are what cause you to be nice rather than real. If you are nice, you won't get blamed or criticized. If you are real, others might see the dark side of your real nature. Then there might be consequences you are unwilling to face—criticism, humiliation, rejection, and abandonment. These are the underlying fears that Satan uses to keep us in the dark. But we know from the Bible that light drives out the dark. Jesus is the light. When you learn to be real without being judgmental, you will see that you can be true to yourself, earn the respect of others, and win with love. You will see that the consequences of false niceness are more severe than those from being real. Furthermore, if you learn to be non-judgmental, you will be able to be real in a way that is *loving*, even if others don't necessarily see you as being "nice."

To be real is the leadership skill of integrity. In its highest form, integrity implies high moral and ethical character. However, in its purest form, integrity happens when you say what you mean and mean what you say—even if others might disagree with you. You are consistent. You are real. Integrity creates trust. You can trust someone who warns they are late for appointments and then delivers on that promise! You might not like it, but you can trust it. The problem is that there are very few such people around. Those who deny it never change. But those who admit it often do something about it. This latter point is the main benefit of being real. You can't change what you can't see, or refuse to admit.

The purpose of this chapter is to give you insights into how to uncover the real you, and what to do when you don't like what you see. You will read six stories about marriage breakdown, being a hypocrite, dealing with annoying habits, arguing and bickering, rage, and lust. Each story is intended to be like watching a short video clip, so that you can fully appreciate the reality of the situation for the characters in the story. From these stories, you will learn:

1. **We make unkind judgments,** everyday, all through the day.
2. **Judging others often gets us the opposite of what we want,** motivating other people to purposely dig in and resist.
3. **Judging others ALWAYS damages our relationships,** breaking down their trust in us and leaving behind a trail of resentment and emotional distance.

2-1 You are Guilty, Not Condemned: Adultery & Separation

No human being can measure up to the standard Jesus set for us. Forgive seventy times seven times, turn the other cheek, give away everything you own to follow Jesus, love your enemy, the last will be first, and and on. A reasonable person can draw only two conclusions from studying the Word:

1. You are guilty.
2. You are not condemned.

It is the second conclusion that makes the first tolerable. Jesus paid the price for your sins on the cross. If you are to become a strong spiritual leader in your home, you must accept this second conclusion deeply and permanently. Otherwise, you will feel a deep shame about the many things you are guilty of having done, are doing, and will do. If you feel ashamed of what you have done, you will put a bowl over your light as surely as a thief hides his crime. However, your crime won't be as blatant as that of the thief. Your crime will be anchored in the sin of being judgmental.

You are only good enough, not perfect. You are a person who embraces his or her imperfection and accepts that you are neither an unworthy worm nor a special God-like warrior. This will happen for you when you are able to accurately see how often you sin, and how incapable you are of not sinning. The rewards to you for actively exploring this truth will be plentiful. You will gain insight and wisdom into how God's values are the mirror opposite of the world's: the meek shall inherit the earth, the last will be first, and the mourners joyous. Indeed, this chapter of *The Non-Judgmental Christian* is primarily about repentance: acknowledging your faults *and releasing your shame and self-judgment*. How do you know if you are a judgmental, shame-filled person? You will have something to hide.

If you are not real within your marriage, you are ripe prey for Satan's temptation for you to be real *outside* your marriage. If that desire happens, the real you will emerge in ways that you might not like. Being real is risky, as your spouse might not like your real thoughts and feelings. However, hiding your truth is even more risky, as this personal story of my adultery and subsequent divorce from my first wife, will reveal.

I was thirty-nine years old, married for ten years, and feeling unhappy with my "successful" life. I had money, wife, career and friends. I did not yet have a spiritual life. It seemed the more successful I became, the more unrest I felt. I kept asking myself the mid-life question, *"Is this all there is?"* Part of me was enjoying the arrival of our new, long awaited and joyously received baby son at home. Yet his arrival also awakened in me an awareness that something was missing from my life. With encouragement from my wife, I decided to take a two month full-time live-in course at a learning institute several hours away from our home. We had both attended it before. There, I had learned one overriding truth about myself: I had a deep need for the approval of others that permeated my every decision. With my wife's support, I signed up in the hope of finally finding myself and getting clear about what kind of work I would enjoy doing for the rest of my life.

When I began the course, all the participants were invited to use nicknames. I chose the name "Adventure," because that was what I wanted. Within the first week, I found myself discovering a dormant, playful side of me thanks to a woman nicknamed Home. A thirty-six-year-old, separated mother of three, she was fun, open and playful. She was bringing out feelings in me that I had not experienced for a long, long time. Soon, Home and I were hanging around quite a bit. I was an exercise fan and she began to join me on my trips into the local gym. I was very open with my wife about this friendship with Home. "She reminds me so much of my sister Diane," I said to her.

During our free time together, I found myself beginning to feel a desire to be alone with Home, which required getting her away from her new boyfriend whom she had just met at the course. I suggested that she and I go to the gym and do a workout, which had become a favorite pastime. Since her boyfriend didn't like to exercise, I felt confident this would do the trick. To my shock, the boyfriend said he would like to come along too. I felt a deep anger, even rage.

When I calmed down, I realized that my intense anger was actually jealousy! I felt as though I would implode if I didn't get what I wanted. I kept reminding myself that I was a happily married man with a four month old baby! That logic did nothing to dissipate how I was feeling. I felt a strong desire for Home and for the first time in many years, I was not able to easily sweep my feelings away. My iron-like discipline over my suppressed real feelings was cracking.

Our relationship continued to heat up over the third week of the course. That weekend, my wife and our son came for their first visit since I had left home. They were not at the hotel as planned and I felt a great deal of anger rise up in me towards her. *Did she screw up again?* I steamed to myself. I began to call various other hotels in the desperate hope that I would find her. To my surprise, she was at the very first hotel that I called. She had just checked in. She said the first hotel wasn't very nice so she decided to find a better one. She had every intention of calling the first hotel and letting me know where they were. She just hadn't had time to do that yet. I grumpily accepted her explanation.

The next night we were out for dinner. I felt punchy. In retrospect, I know I was looking for trouble. Part of the course involved learning how to be authentic—to reveal my truth and not hide it. I was increasingly aware that I had hidden many truths from my wife. One of them was about a long-ago platonic relationship I had before our marriage with a married woman. There was no way I could see a relationship with a married woman working out, and within two months I ended it. I never told my wife about it because I was certain she would be very critical of me. Personally, I was always impressed with myself that I had managed to not cross the line with her.

I felt resentful that I "had" to hide this truth from her for all these years. She had often openly said that she did not want to hear certain things from me. She would tell me, "I just want you to say you like my hair, no matter what you really think." My resentment was now bursting like a cork on a champagne bottle. I decided that I would tell her about this past relationship.

As I expected, she was highly critical of my behavior. I could feel my buried anger come pouring out. I turned around and criticized her in return, sarcastically pointing out how she thought she was so high and mighty. I defiantly defended myself as having done the right thing at the time. She wasn't buying it, and I felt hard done by, as I often did with her. I kissed my son good-bye and we parted company in an angry mood, with ten years of suppressed resentments and anger burning in my chest like a raging fire.

That Sunday was my thirty-ninth birthday. I drove back to my course where Home was waiting for me to go out for a late dinner to celebrate the occasion. The contrast between the playful, supportive Home and the critical wife I had just left behind was like the difference between milk and honey and bitter medicine to me. That night, we steamed up the car until two o'clock in the morning without actually crossing the intercourse line. Two days later, we were in class and our instructor unexpectedly invited a straight-shooting woman nicknamed Harmony to ask someone in the class a "stretch" question. We all knew what that meant. We were about to be asked to explore something we would really rather not talk about.

I immediately felt a strong sense that she was going to ask me about my relationship with Home. A second later, Harmony looked across the room, straight into my eye and said, "Adventure, why are you f——ing around?"

Normally, I would have died right there. But I had just had three weeks of learning about how to be authentic and not hide my truth. I swallowed deeply and said, "I'm not." Bill Clinton would have been proud of me.

The instructor took up the cause. "Well, what are you doing?"

I swallowed hard. I could feel the blood rushing to my face. I simply denied that we had intercourse. My instructor intervened then and asked, "What did you do?"

He then questioned me on every detail of where I put my hand, where she touched me and how I touched her. I answered him in every detail, aware that I was half-numbed out as I survived the trauma of what was happening to me. He challenged my view that I had not crossed "the line" by not having intercourse.

"Who here is feeling judgmental about Adventure's actions right now?" he surveyed the class.

Virtually every hand shot up.

Then it ended. I felt ashamed but not as devastated as I would have expected. I looked over at Home. She hung her head. I glanced over at her boyfriend. He was visibly angry. I had embarrassed him too, I knew that.

Then a realization swept over me. I had just faced my worst fear—to be caught red-handed being bad and to be universally disapproved of. I was in awe that I had survived. This was a liberating moment for me, bad as my behavior was. I knew in my heart that this was the worst thing I had ever done in my life. If the worst thing I had ever done was now public, what did I have left to hide? Nothing. Absolutely nothing. Martin Luther King's words floated into my mind. *Free at last, free at last. Thank God almighty, I'm free at last.* I said a small thank you to myself for Harmony and her life-changing question.

———————————

The path to being non-judgmental is to accept what is real. If you suppress being real, you are giving Satan the fodder he needs to tempt you in your weakest moment. He will use your suppressed judgments and fantasies to lure you into doing things that are destructive to your marriage. Unlike Jesus in the desert, few of us are that strong. The only way out is to be real, before the judgments and fantasies cause you to sin, as I did. Even though I was not a committed believer at the time, let there be no doubt that I knew what I was doing was wrong, adulterous, and carried serious consequences. The problem was that I had ten years of built-up anger and resentments. I was rebelliously breaking out of the cage of my wife's approval and disapproval, a cage I had willingly participated in constructing.

Every judgmental thing my wife had ever said to me came roaring to the front of my mind to justify my actions. I thought of how she refused to have children because she said I was too irresponsible, too unhappy, and worked too many hours. I thought of how I gave up career choices so she could have her career choices, and how she refused to consider living in the country. I thought of the little things that bugged me—her nagging about my slowness in cleaning up the dishes, and not wiping the bathroom mirror clean after flossing my teeth. What played out most strongly in my mind, however, was my pity party about my unfulfilled sexual fantasies. I felt deprived by her. Ultimately, I felt that nothing I did or wanted was ever good enough for her. My wounded pride and suppressed anger came flooding out, blinded by my self-absorbed ego.

With my misdeed being public knowledge, I could not see how I could hide this news from her. I preferred that she heard it from me, rather than from a staff person so I decided to tell her about it that very night, by telephone. She immediately demanded that I leave the course and come home right away. I adamantly refused, assuring her I would not go further with Home. She reluctantly accepted that.

However, my resentments grew. I felt I had finally found a woman who understood me, supported me, and was not critical of my flaws and weaknesses. My sexual fantasies also played out strongly in my mind. The next night, I waited for Home in her room, aware that I was facing a moment of truth. I knew she would go wherever I wanted to go sexually. We had said, "I love you," to each other. I had to decide: *Do I, or don't I?* I thought of my great unhappiness, never feeling good enough, denied of so many things… things I wanted in my life. I decided that I wanted to wreck my marriage, once and for all. When Home arrived, I committed adultery with her. The next day, the first half of the course ended. I drove home and told my wife what I had done. After an emotional day, we separated, never to be together again.

Jesus' words that our judgments come back to us in the measure that we inflict them upon others proved to be prophetic for me. My wife responded to my mean-spirited, weak-kneed destruction of our marriage in kind. Within three weeks, she secretly initiated court action, making up a story that I threatened to kidnap our child and run off to the United States. I arrived at my temporary residence to find a thick legal document pronouncing that she had sole possession of our house, I was barred from coming within four hundred yards of our house, my credit cards were cancelled, and my operating company assets frozen. I would have been absolutely penniless had I not had the good fortune to have withdrawn $20,000 the day before this legal lightning bolt struck me. The measure of my judgments was measured back to me. We set ourselves up for a long, painful two year legal battle that consumed $150,000 in legal fees and many painful emotional struggles.

What I did was wrong. The underlying cause, above all others, was that I had not been real. I hid my truth from my wife. When I left, she was in shock that I had so much anger and resentment towards her. Ten years of passiveness on my part turned into one ugly week of hurtful aggressiveness that ended our marriage in one fell swoop.

God put you together with your spouse for a reason. That reason is to learn how to love. Your partner is perfectly suited for that job. He or she knows exactly what buttons to push to trigger your judgments. For that reason, your spouse is the most dangerous person in the world for you. He or she knows exactly how to hurt you. He or she also knows exactly how to please you. That's why you married him or her.

Your spouse's purpose in your life isn't to make you happy; it is to make you holy. This destiny is part of God's plan for you. He wants you to lean first on Him for your sense of peace and joy, not your wife or husband. When you are nice, you are avoiding the conflict that will help shrink your watermelon and become like a peach. When you are real, you willingly face this danger. His love will feel deeper and closer when you are real and vulnerable in this way.

There is no escaping this lesson. Ten years of avoiding conflicts that my wife and I should have dealt with were instead stored up as resentments that flooded out in much worse forms during our divorce. These continued in my second marriage despite having "done my work" as divorce counselors recommend (and wisely so). If both of you are strongly committed to avoiding conflict, then you are very likely to experience emotional distance and a roommate-like, empty relationship in order to not rock the boat. Either way, being nice will get you in the end. God wants you to be real, to be salt and light. This will be much easier to do if you first focus on being non-judgmental before you act. These words from Paul are an encouragement: "It does not concern me in the least that I be judged by you or any human tribunal; I do not even pass judgment on myself; I am not conscious of anything against me, but I do not thereby stand acquitted; the one who judges me is the Lord." (1 CO 4:3-4 NAB)

Group Study: Real Lesson 2-1: Get comfortable revealing your past mistakes. With people you trust, work on being non-judgmental about these past deeds and how others might react to your news. You need to accept, repent, and know you are forgiven by God. Do this in a safe place with a trusted friend, or join a small group. Then go to your loved one, tell them your truth and accept his or her reaction, without judgment and with compassion. Know that you have a loving intention, even if your wife, for example, thinks that she would have rather not known your truth. Your truth has God's purpose for her in it too. Get expert help if necessary to coach you and help her. You will know you've succeeded if you can laugh at yourself, or at least, comfortably admit your mistakes.

NOTES

2-2 We Are Hypocrites: Father, Son & Yogurt

Judgments are like a snowball. They stick to you. As time rolls along, the snowball becomes a boulder and then an avalanche, as happened in my first marriage. The antidote to this is to notice your judgments right when they happen and deal with them quickly and humbly. In this following example, we see an example of a man who notices his own hypocrisy. Hypocrisy is a major cause of being judgmental. Hypocrites have a different set of rules for themselves than for others, just as the Pharisees did in Jesus' time. We have that different set of rules because of pride, which is the cause of all judgments. We believe we are special, deserving, and above the rules. Jesus teaches us that real love is the opposite— that we are servants, meekly putting ourselves last and others first. This goes against our ego and inflames our pride. Noticing that this is true for you will give you the courage to melt the snowballs as they come, eliminating your own resentments and those of others day by day, moment by moment.

In this story, we read about a father who is caught being a hypocrite by his young son, and what he decides to do about it.

Josh opened the fridge door. School had just ended and he was a hungry nine year old boy. His eye caught the last single serving container of yogurt, one of his favorite foods. He looked up at his dad, who happened to be standing there.

"Can I have that yogurt?"

Dad hesitated. He thought of the high cost of that particular brand of yogurt, and how handy they were for the kids' lunches. "You know Josh, I'd really rather you didn't. Those little containers are perfect for lunch and if you eat them all at home, we'll have nothing left for school tomorrow."

"Oh-h, okay," Josh said, hanging his head in disappointment.

"How about this apple… or a banana?" Dad offered brightly.

"Ah-h. No thanks."

That weekend, mom and dad went out Saturday night to a dinner party. As usual, dad came home feeling bloated from all that good food, eaten late into the night. The next morning, he got out of bed, showered and headed for the kitchen. "*Hm-m, what do I want for breakfast,*" he thought to himself. He looked over his choices as he scanned the fridge. "*Frozen waffle? Nah-h. Too bland. Make an egg? Nah-h. Too much effort. Toast? Nah-h. Too filling. Ah ha! There's a yogurt left. That might be just right—not too filling but enough to get me going."* He reached in and picked up the yogurt. Then he ripped off the foil lid, grabbed a spoon and headed for the living room to watch TV with the kids.

He had eaten the second spoonful when suddenly Josh piped up.

"Hey! I thought you said those yogurts were only for lunches!"

Dad felt flat-footed, caught, yet somehow feeling like this was different. He thought fast. "Well, I don't eat lunches away from home, so I eat them here," Dad responded lamely, rationalizing his answer based on his work-at-home career.

"Oh," said Josh, without argument.

The weight of his son's silent acceptance of dad's explanation wasn't lost on dad.

He stewed about it for the rest of the day. He knew he had set a bad example, with one set of rules for himself, and a different set for the kids. *"Well,"* he thought, *"I'm not a kid and doesn't rank have its privileges?"* It sounded good when he said it to himself, but he didn't feel convinced.

That night, he thought it over. *"I really don't like the example I've set. I've got to do something."* He thought about his options. *"I could just say, Okay, I was wrong, and I won't have yogurts anymore either. Hm-m-m. How does that idea sit?,"* he asked himself. *"Not well! I want yogurt from time to time. I guess one option is to give all the kids the same privilege!"*

The next morning, he spoke to Josh. "Josh, do you remember when you saw me eating yogurt in the living room yesterday morning and you said, "Hey I thought those were only for lunches?"

"Yeah, I remember…" Josh looked a bit wary as if to say, "Am I in trouble?"

"Well, I thought about it," said his dad, "and I think you were right. I did make two different rules and in this case, I think that was wrong of me. You can have all the yogurt you want from now on, okay?"

"Okay!" Josh responded happily.

Dad looked at his son with a warm smile. *"Sometimes, eating humble pie feels really good,"* he thought.

As you become more focused on being non-judgmental, you will begin to see the many ways in which you and I are hypocrites. Jesus spoke harshly towards the teachers of the law for this. "Jesus replied, 'And you experts in the law, woe to you, because you load people down with burdens they can hardly carry, and you yourselves will not lift one finger to help them" (LK 11:46 NIV) In this situation, Dad demonstrated one solution to dealing with hypocrisy—eat humble pie. This kind of leadership leaves a lasting impression on those we love. Dads can be wrong and dads can admit their error and make up for it, quickly and without shame.

Did you notice the speed with which the nine year old boy noticed his father's hypocrisy? That is how judgments work. Dad declares a "rule." Then his loved ones begin looking to see if he walks his own talk. When he fails, they are quick to be judgmental about him. His lack of integrity is instantly apparent. This happened to me recently at my Toastmasters club, a speaking organization to which I belong. Our speakers were going over their time limits that evening. At the end of the meeting, I spoke up and said that in the professional speaker circuit that I frequent, the veterans are adamant that "professional speakers always finish on time, no matter what." The very next week, I was giving an evaluation of another person's speech. I went over my three and a half minute time limit by a full minute. Not one but *two* people came up to me afterwards to point out how they couldn't help but think of how I was violating my own loud declaration from the week before!

If you were perfect, you would always do what you said you would do, and live up to your own good intentions. But you are not, and neither am I. That's why becoming comfortable with your imperfection is so important. Otherwise, you will feel ashamed of yourself when you get caught. Your shame will cause you to instantly want to deny, cover up or rationalize your actions. And I guarantee you will find a way to do it! In my speaking example above, I could have rationalized and justified my hypocrisy in three ways:

1. I was giving an evaluation, not making a speech, giving me an escape based on a technicality;
2. the speech I was evaluating was double the length of the usual speech, making it harder to evaluate it in the same amount of time;
3. I had asked the chairperson for more time and was turned down.

Thanks to years of the Lord's real-life training in this area, I did not feel an impulse to get defensive with these excuses. I simply agreed that I blew it. Interestingly, my critics immediately began justifying my action for me! One quickly commented on how long the speech was that I was evaluating. The other person acknowledged that I had asked for more time and should have been given that time. I felt a warm peace when they responded in that way. These are the moments that affirm to me that if we do not judge, we will not be judged in return. Indeed, we will be loved in return. But we have to love them first, by not denying our real, hypocritical selves.

St. Paul points out our hypocritical nature when he writes, "You, therefore, have no excuse, you who pass judgment on someone else, for at whatever point you judge the other, you are condemning yourself, because you who pass judgment do the same things" (RO 2:1 NIV) I call this phenomenon, *"All I See is Me."* Every judgment you have of a person, a situation or a behavior is either something you do yourself, or would do if you let yourself be who you *really* are. A father tells his son not to have a yogurt at home, and then has one himself. I tell speakers not to go overtime, then do it myself. Let me illustrate with another example. A man is a smoker. Through sheer willpower, he quits. As he conquers the habit, he starts to become an outspoken anti-smoker! Why is he such an adamant anti-smoker? It is because underneath all that judgmental anti-smoking talk is a smoker aching to light one up! His judgments of smokers and smoking are his way of suppressing his *own* desire to smoke. Indeed, this is one of the core reasons we are afraid to be non-judgmental. Our judgments are our way of controlling ourselves! The anti-smoker is actually speaking to himself, loudly reminding himself that smoking is a bad thing. This explains why the stereotyped TV evangelist who rants and raves against pornography is the one who gets caught in a motel room with a prostitute. Underneath his ranting and raving is a man desperate for raw sex.

If you want to eliminate your judgments of others, the easiest way is to notice your judgments and ask yourself, "In what way is this true of me?" The path is really quite straightforward. Every judgment you have of anyone else, for any reason, is linked to a belief you have that says, "My way is more right than your way." Even if that happens to be true, as long as you attach a "judgment" to it, you will be blinded by the plank in your eye.

An example happened to me at Easter dinner. Thirteen of the adults in my family were gathered around my sister's dining room table, enjoying turkey and ham. I piped up at one point to announce the news that my ex-wife's aunt just died. I described the family's shock when they found out she literally had one day to live. She had just enough time to say good bye to her loved ones, then fell into a coma and passed away less than twenty four hours later. My father immediately responded by telling a story about someone he knew who found out he had cancer and died within two weeks. I thought to myself, "There goes Dad again, trying to one-up the other guy's story." I didn't feel critical, just aware that he was doing it. A few minutes later, my sister mentioned a Christian concert of a great pianist that she planned to attend. Did any of us want to join her? Without responding to her question, I immediately began to describe a Christian concert that I planned to attend. I went on to describe the event in great detail, with its two hundred person choir and my friend the conductor who had studied music at the university level for twelve years and owned a piano/organ store and how magnificently he played a three keyboard organ and... you get the point? Finally, I came back to her and asked her, "So tell me more about this pianist you're going to see?" But for the grace of God, the "old" me would never have even noticed that I had just done the *very act* that I noticed my father doing just minutes earlier.

Group Study: Real Lesson 2-2: Practice ALL I SEE IS ME. Notice your judgments about others and test yourself to see whether you yourself say and do the very same things. Driving your car is an excellent place to do this. Take note of when another driver irritates you. Then watch to see if you do the very same thing, or find yourself suppressing your desire to do the same thing. If you are studying this in a small group, think of one annoying habit that your wife, child, boss or co-worker has. Can you imagine that some part of you has this same habit, or would, if you were to let yourself be completely real?

NOTES

2-3 Dealing With Their Annoying Habits: The Cell Phone

When you are real, you deal with your unhappiness as it happens, without undue delay. When you do, your judgments about others will emerge, and they will react. Then you will both have to deal with it. *How* you deal with it will reflect whether you are coming from a loving, surrendered place, or a fearful, controlling place. In this story, you will see how a man who is real allows his judgments about a small irritant to come right back at him according to the measure by which he judges others. This story reveals that we use judgments to try to change the way other people behave. However, if you start paying attention, you will see that judgments often get us exactly the opposite of what we want!

———————

He kissed his wife as he was about to leave the house. It was six A.M., and he was making a two and a half hour drive to deliver a one day workshop. "Remember to leave your phone on tonight, okay honey?" he said across the hallway. "Just in case I get back early and can meet you and the kids somewhere." She intended to be out that night with the kids, taking them to their various activities from six o'clock right until nine P.M.

When the day ended, he jumped into his car and eagerly dialed her cell phone. The annoying nasal voice of the operator answered. "The customer you have dialed is currently not available. Please try again later." Disappointed, he hung up. Maybe she temporarily turned it off, he thought. I'll try again later.

Thirty minutes later, he hit "resend." He waited expectantly as it rang once, then twice. Then it picked up. "The customer you have dialed is currently not available..." He hit the End key. Why the heck doesn't she have the phone on? he thought with some frustration. He replayed that morning's conversation in his mind when he asked her to keep her cell phone on. He was certain she had understood and agreed. He felt annoyed. "I'll try again in a while," he thought.

An hour later, he tried again. No answer again. He looked at the clock on his car dashboard. It glowed "6:45" in green digits. He made a decision to call his parents instead, maybe even drop in and visit them. They were home so he agreed to stop in for a visit.

He tried his wife one more time just before he arrived at his parents. No answer. He could feel his annoyance grow. "I can't believe she forgot to turn on her phone…again!" This had been an issue for them a few times in the past, ever since they bought the "family" package of two phones. "I've got to stay cool," he thought to himself. "Who knows why she doesn't have it on—could be any of a hundred reasons." Giving himself a familiar little pep talk, he reminded himself, "I only get myself in trouble when I make assumptions and leap to conclusions. I've got to just ask her what happened, and leave it at that." He sighed as he anticipated walking that fine line of asking about it without seeming like he was accusing her of anything.

When he arrived home, the house was dark. He began shoveling the snow off the driveway when she pulled in with the kids. Once inside, he hugged her and gave each of the kids a warm hello. She piled groceries onto the kitchen counter top. After asking about her day, she said, "We tried to call you."

"Oh," he said, somewhat surprised. Then he felt mildly irritated. "That's odd. My phone was on the whole time."

"No, I mean we called you here at home."

"I was in my car," he said, the edge in his voice beginning to show. How could she not have remembered I was driving? he asked himself critically.

"I know," she said. "We only tried around eight o'clock. I thought you might have been home by then."

"Oh," he grunted. His mind shifted gears. "How did you call me, anyway? I tried your cell phone several times but it wasn't on."

"I used Emily's phone. Mine didn't work. It's right there," she said, looking mildly embarrassed as she pointed to a cell phone lying plugged into the wall. "The battery died so I couldn't take it along. I plugged it in for the day instead."

He felt the niggle again. This time it had an edge to it. He remembered how often this happened with her. He would try to call her, but she would forget to charge the phone. He thought to himself, "You'd think she'd make it a habit to recharge the battery after having the phone for nearly two years, and using it on a daily basis." Suddenly, the words spilled out, before he could stop himself. "I sometimes wonder why we even *bother* having a second cell phone."

An angry look flashed across her face. "You know what! Just get rid of it. I am tired of all the grief you give me over that phone."

He was momentarily stunned. The velocity of her reaction, and the finality of it startled him. He thought with some defensiveness, "I have only ever said anything about three times!" He resisted the urge and with some self-control said, "Okay. We can do that if you want." He turned away silently. Collecting his thoughts, he came back to her a few moments later. "I think what bothers me is that I specifically asked you to keep the phone on tonight."

"Well I couldn't," she said evenly. "The battery died."

They went about putting away the groceries quietly, while the kids played up and down the kitchen and hallway. "Let it go," he thought to himself. "She'll probably change her mind in the morning when she cools down."

What did this husband want from his wife? He wanted her commitment to charge the battery and to keep the cell phone turned on. Instead, his judgmental response got the exact opposite response! Now, she wouldn't have a cell phone on *ever*. He let his real judgments about her behavior slip out, despite his best intentions to not let that happen. "Why do we even bother having a second cell phone?" spoken with a touch of sarcasm, was a judgmental comment designed to make her feel guilty. She felt his condemnation and reacted swiftly with a response designed to end his judgments, not solve the problem. He was real. Now he had to deal with it.

It is never too late to deal with a situation you have inflamed by being judgmental. Remember, the alternative is false niceness brewing in the form of resentments. Resentments are small bricks made up of judgments that create emotional walls between you and your loved one. If you want to live a lonely, isolated, unhappy life, false niceness is a sure-fire way to rob yourself of His peace and their love. Being real, even if you are judgmental, forces you to deal with it... now!

You must begin by being non-judgmental about the judgment that comes flinging back in your face. In this example, the husband's judgment about his wife's cell phone habits instantly came back at him. He must break the judgment cycle by not counter-judging her. He can do this if he can accept that she is entitled to be judgmental if she wants to be. To be non-judgmental is to set her free, and that means she is also free to be judgmental, just as Jesus set you free to be judgmental.

Once he is accepting of her decision, and is not taking it personally, he can act wisely. In this case, this husband asked his wife the next morning if she was serious about canceling the cell phone. He felt confident she was making an impulsive decision because she relied on the cell phone on her many travels with the children's activities. To his surprise, she replied without hesitating, "Yes!"

"Why?" he asked, centering himself by accepting her right to stick to her position. "It seems like a handy device that you've used a lot."

She hesitated. His open-ended question drew her in as it often did. She looked up at him. "It's because I feel like you are always trying to keep control of me with that phone." He'd learned enough to know that even if he didn't like this answer, it was honest and real.

"Really!" he responded. "Do you think I chase you down that often?" resisting the urge to say that in his own opinion, he did not.

"No-o," she hesitated. "You don't chase me down. I just feel like I have to always have that phone on. I even say to my co-workers, 'Oh oh, I forgot to turn on my phone! My husband is going to be so angry with me!'"

He breathed deep, not allowing himself to get hooked by this new piece of information that she made him out to be an angry, controlling husband to her co-workers. "Do you feel that I get angry with you? I can't recall getting angry..."

"Yeah, well, maybe not angry, but you don't like it."

"Well, that's true," he admitted.

"Anyway," she continued, "I'd just rather not have the darn thing anymore."

"Okay..." his voice drifted off. He was surprised at the conviction in her decision. He had been quite certain she would cool down and keep the phone. He decided to accept her decision without trying to talk her out of it. "We'll see what happens as time goes by." He called the phone company and put the phone on temporary suspension of services.

Two months later, she asked him to turn the phone back on. She missed the convenience of the cell phone, and felt the effect of numerous miscommunications that were now happening as a result. She asked him without shame or regret. He agreed to do it and when she got home that night, her face lit up as she gave him a great hug!

There are three lessons here worth noting. The first is that by being non-judgmental, the man created a safe space for his wife to open up and admit her truth. As is often the case with anyone who is upset, her truth was full of judgments: he was controlling, angry, and caused her anxiety at work. The second aspect of this leadership moment worth noting was that he resisted the temptation to get "hooked" by her judgments. In so doing, she took ownership of them and actually tempered them quite a bit, admitting he wasn't really angry, nor did he really "chase" her down all the time. This is a crucial benefit of not being judgmental yourself—it reduces the judgments of others towards you. The third insight from this leadership moment was that he did not try to pressure her into doing things his way, even though he very much wanted her to keep using the cell phone. To win with love means to respect the boundaries of other people, and their right to make their own choices, even if you are negatively affected.

By not arguing, selling, or pressuring her to take on the phone, he left the door wide open for her to change her mind, based on her own practical real-world experiences in the coming days and weeks. If he had tried to pressure her, which is the strongest practical evidence that a person is being judgmental, she would have very likely deepened her resolve to not get "pushed" into using the phone, just as I refused to clean up the dishes or wipe the bathroom mirror for ten years!

Most relationship struggles are a battle for control. By being real, each of you in the relationship will learn what is within your rights and what is not. The hands on the front cover of this book reflect the "steady hands" of Jesus. When you are non-judgmental, you learn to support the right of others to do things their way, while resisting people who try to pressure you in areas that belong to you. We will look at this in more depth in Lesson Four, where you learn how to wisely influence loved ones to change, freely and willingly.

Paul wrote, "Do nothing out of selfish ambition or vain conceit, but in humility consider others better than yourselves" (PH 2:3 NIV). To be a strong leader, you require large doses of humility—the humility to admit your mistakes, and the humility to allow other people to make their own choices even if you think you know better. The real test comes when time passes and you are proven to be right. Your ability to not refrain from saying "I told you so" will be massively strengthened by the fact that you never "told you so" in the first place! Then she will decide of her own free will, for her own reasons, and all you will have done is created the space and permission for her to do so with honor and grace. In this way, you will be holding her "holy and blameless." For what is blame? It is judgment. To be blameless is to be without judgment, without fault. She is making the best decision she can for herself, for her own reasons, no matter what you think.

Group Study: Real Lesson 2-3: Identify an annoying behavior change you want from a loved one. Does the person know how you feel? If he or she doesn't, why not? What are you afraid would happen if you were real and honest with the person? Intentionally explore the possibility that what you fear will indeed happen. Can you accept that possibility? If you struggle with being real, consider further study using the book, *What's Important Now*, by John Kuypers. It contains six practical strategies for being real, without being judgmental.

NOTES

_____

_____

_____

_____

_____

2-4 Arguing and Bickering: The Missing Clothes

As you become more real, you will notice that you set yourself up for failure by making judgments that are assumptions based on your past experiences. Judgments are your past re-surfacing in the present moment. You are not actually "seeing" what is real. You are seeing a replay of the past, and are assuming that this situation is a repeat of a similar past situation. The result is that you will jump to conclusions, make wrong accusations, and hurt the ones you love. In this story, you will learn how your judgments lead to misunderstandings caused by making assumptions that are not real.

He awoke at 5:15 A.M., feeling groggy but awake. His son's hockey practice began at six A.M. and they had a twenty minute drive ahead of them. Once he had the boy up and dressed, he remembered that he wanted to bring his son's dirty clothes along to his ex-wife's house, where he would be dropping off his son after practice. He quietly tiptoed back into the boys' bedroom so as not to awaken his step-son who lay silently sleeping. The closet door creaked and he groped around in the usual place for the large pile of clothes that lay there yesterday. Nothing there.

He carefully closed the door and then reached under the bed to check another favorite place to keep dirty clothing. Nothing there either. Mystified, he guessed that his wife had already gathered up the clothes and put them down in the laundry room herself. He padded down the two flights to the basement to rifle through the laundry baskets, the washing machine itself and the dryer. Nothing.

He went back upstairs and glanced at the clock. 5:30 A.M. It was time to go. Mildly frustrated, he gave up on the clothes, gathered up his son and the equipment and off they went.

That night, his wife briefly stepped inside the house, before heading out to her exercise class. He asked her quickly if she knew where the dirty clothes were.

"They're right there!" she exclaimed, pointing to a black plastic bag full of clothes leaning against the wall.

"You're kidding," he responded in shock.

"They were sitting right here on the kitchen table this morning. Didn't you see it?"

"No," he said, immediately feeling a bit dumb. "I looked high and low for them. I checked the closet, under the bed... I even checked the laundry room!"

"I can't believe you didn't see the bag. It was right there. Didn't you notice that it was full of clothes?" she asked with a note of incredulity.

He began to feel his defenses rise. "No-o. I didn't see it. You often have bags of stuff lying around and I just assumed it was one of yours. Why would I think to look for his clothes in a plastic bag on the kitchen table?"

She rolled her eyes. "Well, it was sitting right there. I can't believe you couldn't see that it was full of his clothes." The scornful tone in her voice was not lost on him, and he bit.

"Telling me that I should have seen the bag in such a condescending tone isn't helpful to me," he retorted.

Her face flushed instantly. "I'm leaving," she said in a low voice, looking down at the floor. She opened the door and marched off to her exercise class.

What went wrong here? Two people with the best of intentions quickly slid into an unhappy place. She was trying to be helpful, anticipating his desire to bring the dirty clothes over to his ex-wife's and gathering them up. He was trying his best to find the clothes in order to do exactly that. Instead, the conversation spun into one of blame. He implied that his failure to find the clothes was her fault, because she had handled the clothes in a way that was different from the usual routine. She implied that his failure to find the clothes was his fault because he had failed to see the bag lying so obviously under his nose.

Of course, both were right in their own way. It was the desire to find fault and the resulting blaming that caused this ordinary situation to crumble into an unhappy, judgmental moment. One judgment led to a second one, and the cycle was off and running.

Either person can take the lead and break this cycle at any time. The most effective way to do so is to accept the judgment of the other person. "Yes, honey, you're right. I screwed up. I must be blind. How could I not have seen the bag, sitting right there underneath my nose?" This requires humility. You must own your mistake without wanting to point out their mistake. In this way, you show your leadership through the ability to freely and willingly acknowledge your sinful, imperfect, real self.

Humility requires a strong sense of self-worth. Humility is a character trait that Jesus exhibited completely. Paul describes Jesus' humility like this: "Your attitude should be the same as that of Christ Jesus: Who, being in very nature God, did not consider equality with God something to be grasped, but made himself nothing, taking the very nature of a servant, being made in human likeness. And being found in appearance as a man, he humbled himself and became obedient to death—even death on a cross! Therefore God exalted him to the highest place and gave him the name that is above every name." (PH 2:6-9 NIV)

When you are non-judgmental, you take on the role of providing spiritual leadership in your home. You take the hit first, just as Jesus did, paying the price for our sins without any strings attached. Jesus made himself nothing. When you are nothing, you will have everything that matters—love! When you love in this way, you will have leadership moments that will almost certainly result in your loved ones *also* responding in an opposite way. "Well, don't be so hard on yourself honey. I can understand not seeing the bag. I know it was five-thirty in the morning and you weren't expecting me to have put the bag together like that." This is a response filled with compassion and empathy, instead of guilt and shame. What man wouldn't want that kind of response from his wife? You can get it, if you can give it yourself first.

Of course, his wife could have done the same. When he explained how he had no reason to think of looking into that particular bag, she could have said, "Yes, honey, I can understand that. It was so early in the morning and I do often have other things packed in bags here at the front door." That would be non-judgmental leadership on her part. But you can't *make* her do that. You can only control how you respond, not how she responds. This is why being non-judgmental is humbling.

Either person in a relationship *always* has the opportunity to break the judgment cycle. Whoever does so is the one demonstrating spiritual leadership. We can only do so if we are able to come from a place of love. St. Paul inspires us in this way when he writes: "Do everything without complaining or arguing, so that you become **blameless** and pure, children of God without fault in a crooked and depraved generation in which you shine like stars in the universe as you hold out the word of life—in order that I may boast on the day of Christ that I did not run or labor for nothing" (PH 2:14-16 NIV).

Anyone can get sucked into the vortex of judgment and blame. When you focus on being real, you begin to notice the conversations in your head that are the fodder for judgment. You see how you are making assumptions based on your past experiences that lead you down the slippery slope of harboring preconceived judgments. These lie like landmines, just waiting for your loved one to say or do something that you think confirms your suspicion. Then you pounce before you can help yourself.

Non-judgmental leaders notice these thoughts, and turn the tide away from blame and shame and towards compassion and love. Someone must take that lead, and St. Paul says that person is the husband. This is a huge responsibility. No man can do this alone, but only with by the grace of the Holy Spirit. "I can do all things through Christ who strengthens me," wrote Paul in Philippians 4:13 (NIV). The reward for the man who willingly takes the leadership role in these small moments is peace and joy, both for himself and for his wife.

Group Study: Real Lesson 2-4: Commit to being the first to admit your role in a conflict. Make it your goal to be the *first* to catch yourself being wrong, making a mistake, or being judgmental. Be quick to own it, before your loved one has a chance to point it out to you (which they will!). Notice your thoughts when you *know* you are in the wrong, but don't want to admit it. Don't judge yourself for your weakness. Go to Jesus who always forgives you, and who will strengthen you for the next time. You are imperfect, and He loves you anyway.

NOTES

2-5 Rage: Real Men have Real Feelings

The real you probably has some rage buried in you somewhere. You'll know it is true if you have a hard time getting in touch with your feelings. I had a boss who once said to me, "John, you need to be more of a chameleon. You speak the same way in the same tone whether you have exciting news or terrible news." I was quite struck by his feedback at the time. It was only when I let people get closer to the real me that I began to get in touch with my suppressed rage. In the end, I learned that the only way we can truly be non-judgmental and present-moment focused is to get rid of the layers of our "false" self under which lay who we really are. The path to being real is blocked by hurts from our past. Our judgments are like walls that protect us from experiencing these hurts again. You will know this is true if certain situations trigger you emotionally in a deep way. Like a knot in your neck muscle, they hurt when touched and you will instantly want to blame the person triggering you or get away from them as fast as possible.

The first time I became aware that the real me was buried was on a course my first wife and I attended. This is what happened. On our first evening, the instructor asked us what we hoped to accomplish by coming to this course. I put up my hand. "I've read both books and I've learned a tremendous amount. I've gotten so much from them alone that if I get nothing at all this weekend, I'll still be thrilled!" Inside, I was excited to be there, like a kid who is thoroughly prepared for his exams. "Bring on the test! I'm ready to ace this course!" In fact, I had decided that some of this stuff might be useful in my management consulting and organizational change work. I had my notebook in hand, and I began taking copious notes about the techniques and processes the instructor was using. Unwittingly, I stopped being a participant and fell into my familiar role as an outside observer.

About an hour later, the instructor asked us to pair off with someone. I looked around and my eyes met with a middle-aged blonde woman. We smiled at each other and agreed to work together. The instructor asked us to take two minutes to share a little bit about ourselves. Susan[1] was a doctor from New York. She had been married for twenty-seven years. In the next breath, she said she had also been having a long-term affair with another man for many years. She felt racked with guilt. She was here hoping to get some clarity on whether to stay in her marriage or leave her husband for her lover. "*Wow*," I thought with the naiveté of a country boy, "*people actually do this kind of stuff.*"

Then we were asked to close our eyes and concentrate on the other person. "Hold their hands," the instructor soothingly requested. "*This is getting a little weird,*" I thought as I held Susan's aging hands rather awkwardly. I kept expecting her to pull away but she didn't, so I continued to go along with the exercise.

---

1 Details have been changed to protect her privacy

The instructor continued. "Imagine what those hands have accomplished, what they've been through, what moments they've shared with others." I pictured a scalpel in her hands, slicing open somebody's body. Her fingers were short and stubby, with some aging spots on the back of her hands. "*Kind of unattractive,*" I thought.

The instructor intervened again. "Even though you don't know this person, can you feel some love for them?" "*Not really,*" I thought. "*This is a bit strange if you ask me.*" Then the instructor asked us to open our eyes and look directly into the eyes of the person sitting across from us. "Imagine their positives and how perfect they are. Can you let go of any judgments that you may have formed about your partner already?"

As I looked into Susan's eyes, I felt very uncomfortable. Suddenly, I felt an uncontrollable urge to laugh. I held it back with all of my might. A moment later, I began to feel very angry. "*What a bunch of crap this is!*" I felt furious. "*I don't know this person from Adam! How can I think she's perfect? What are these people trying to do to me, anyway!*" Then I went numb. I was no longer able to connect with Susan or to follow the instructor's directions. My mind went into a kind of paralysis as I stared blankly at her. I went into survival mode, shut down but still alive. After what seemed like a long time, the exercise ended. Our instructor asked us if everyone felt a connection, a moment of love for the other person. Almost everyone put up their hand. Except me. Even my wife put up her hand, I noticed.

I thought over my experience. I remembered a brief connection when Susan's eyes got watery. Then came that crazy desire to laugh. I remembered once laughing in the face of my Grade Three teacher, while she was angry with me. Then came the anger, even rage. I was in shock over that. Why was I so furious? Finally, the numbness came. I felt afraid, even terrified. Looking in Susan's eyes had scared the daylights out of me! The awareness stunned me. I realized that the real me was afraid to be intimate.

That night, my wife and I discussed this dramatic event. I was aware enough to notice that my intention to be an observer of their teaching methods was further proof of my fear of intimacy. I saw that I really lived my life as an observer, watching myself like some kind of protective angel, filtering every event and "deciding" how to be in response to it rather than just being the real me. I wrote in my journal, "*I know it must mean that I don't trust myself at all! I find it so tough to live in the present as a result. Whenever my alter ego and me start to come together, I become very conscious of it and I pull away, stopping it from happening. I really notice this when I'm doing my meditation. I notice that my thoughts have stopped and I start thinking about that. Next thing I know, my mind is racing with thoughts again. This also probably explains why I have such a poor memory and am a relatively poor listener."*

The fear of our rage emerging is one of the main reasons many people choose to be "nice." At least that way, they don't go somewhere they might not be able to control. As my understanding of this grew, I became increasingly committed to connecting with my real feelings. I began to see a therapist. He explained that his goal would be to help me feel my feelings in a controlled, safe way. What I liked was that he really didn't want to analyze my feelings to death. He simply wanted to help me feel the feelings, without being afraid of them.

I joined his men's group where each of us was seeking to be more real, more loving, and happier in our personal lives. Some of the men had experienced serious sexual abuse and drug and alcohol abuse. Some were like me, sorting out broken personal lives. All of them were real, frank, and supportive. This group of men was the safest, most supportive, and helpful I had ever been with in my life. No topic was off-limits, including sexual fantasies, extramarital affairs, drugs, fighting, failing, falling off the bandwagon, feeling angry or merely having a self-pity party.

One day, I was struggling in the midst of my long and expensive divorce battle. Connecting to my feelings was still rare for me and my therapist was quick to recognize when I was numbing out. That day, in the men's group, he asked me if I would do an experiment. I agreed. He asked me to lay down on the floor. Then he asked if four of the guys would volunteer to hold me down, one man on each of my limbs. Each man readily agreed. He went over and closed the curtains, just in case someone was to peek in and misunderstand what was happening. Then he told me to try to get up, while he asked the guys to hold me down.

As their powerful arms clamped down on limbs, my fury unleashed. How I wanted to be free! I fought and kicked and screamed and yelled, twisting and turning like a madman, ripping one guys shirt while burning up with rage and anger. After a minute, my therapist asked us to stop. We immediately stopped.

"How do you feel?" he asked me.

I was breathing hard. "Fine," I said through gritted teeth. I looked up at my four captors. Each was red-faced and sweating.

"Let's keep going then," he said.

If I was raging the first time, I doubled it. My fury knew no bounds. I twisted and turned, trying to free myself from eight powerful arms holding me down with all their might. My head lashed forward, trying to bite one guy's arm. After nearly two minutes, I gave up. I was spent.

I cry even now as I write this. These men gave me a gift. I felt such a release, such a lifting of a burden I had carried for a long time. I was so afraid of my feelings up until then. I was so afraid that if I let my feelings out of their cage, I would not be able to control myself. That day, I let my rage explode at every injustice I ever felt in my life, especially in my divorce. I discovered the humbling truth that my anger neither changed the world, nor did it turn me into an axe murderer.

Rage is one way we express our judgments. Our pride and ego are hurt. We are convinced we deserve more, and ask how can "they" do this to us. Nowhere is this more true than when someone triggers feelings within you that you don't want to feel. You will automatically want to strike out at the person as the cause of your pain. This is false, ego-based thinking. Another person can't make you feel anything. You are doing that all by yourself. The person's behavior is merely the trigger. When you feel angry if he or she is critical, fails to keep a commitment, misbehaves, interrupts you, rejects your ideas, or embarrasses you, that is your evidence that the real you is judgmental. You want to control people, change them, and make them be the way you want them to be.

For the purpose of this book, the key lesson here is to notice that your rage is real. You cannot be non-judgmental if you are afraid to connect with your real feelings. You will unconsciously and automatically keep up your façade as a "nice" person, not a real person. You will feel ill at ease and uncomfortable when things get emotional. In those moments, you are numbed out, afraid that people might see and judge the real you, or that you might see and judge them!

This is so important because you cannot feel love if you cannot feel anger. Emotions come in a package. The person who laughs easily loves easily, and is also in touch with his or her anger. The person who has the fake smile pasted on, or is robot-like about their feelings, will have a difficult time feeling emotionally connected. The result will be relationships that are distant, roommate-like, and not real.

If you find it difficult to connect to your feelings, you can be sure that the real you is buried underneath a mountain of judgments that you have suppressed over the course of twenty, forty or sixty years. Your only way out is to feel them for real. This will happen more easily when you accept John's words, "If we say, "We are without sin," we deceive ourselves, and the truth is not in us. If we acknowledge our sins, he is faithful and just and will forgive our sins and cleanse us from every wrongdoing. If we say, "We have not sinned," we make him a liar, and his word is not in us. (1 JOHN 1:8-10 NAB) The key is to find a safe place to express your real feelings in order that the Lord may cleanse your sinful self.

Group Study: Real Lesson 2-5: What is happening in your life that you feel angry about? Can you find someone who will listen to you without giving you any advice, and just let you rant and rave? What judgments are underneath your rage? Who is "doing it" to you, and how? What prideful beliefs are you holding that say you deserve more than what you are getting? In what way are you angry with yourself for having allowed this situation to have happened in the first place?

NOTES

2-6 Lust: How to Make Your Wife Your Dream Woman

Jesus said in Matthew 19:4-6,"Have you not read that from the beginning the Creator 'made them male and female' and said, 'For this reason a man shall leave his father and mother and be joined to his wife, and the two shall become one flesh'? So they are no longer two, but one flesh. Therefore, what God has joined together, no human being must separate." (NAB) Becoming one flesh with your wife involves much more than mere intercourse. You are being extremely vulnerable with her. You are merging who you are with who she is. "Self" disappears. Your conscious, analytical, thinking mind disappears. You lose yourself in her, and she loses herself in you. This is blissful sexuality as God intended, deeply spiritual, emotionally electrifying, and physically ecstatic.

If this description seems like it only happens in the movies and not in your real world, there is probably one good reason. Judgments. Judgments are the cause of fantasizing. At some level, the perfect sexual experience with the perfect mate is out there. You feel incomplete, which is a judgment that says your wife (or husband) isn't good enough. You deserve more—more frequency, more variety, more intensity, more pleasure!

Judgments also bring about the opposite effect. Perhaps you are no longer interested in sex. All the judgments have made your relationship unsafe. Problems in the bedroom are rooted in problems in the kitchen. If your wife does not feel emotionally safe, she will have a difficult time letting herself go sexually with you. The same is true for you. Erectile dysfunction is in many cases due to a man not feeling emotionally safe with his wife. I experienced this when I was divorced, unsaved and having sex with the woman I was dating. Suddenly, I had trouble ejaculating! This never happened even once while I was married. I realized that I was unable to completely let go during sex. I began having performance-related thoughts such as, "*Will I be able to? What if I can't? I've got to succeed this time.*" These are judgmental self-doubts focused on whether you are "good enough."

Feeling self-conscious is the evidence that at some level, you do not feel safe. If you are to be real with your partner about this, you must overcome any sense of shame you feel about these truths. Nor must you blame your wife as the cause, even though her judgments of you will definitely contribute to your inability to fully let go with her. Noticing these real thoughts simply means you must learn how to create safeness within yourself, as well as for her. Non-judgment will accomplish both of these goals, and you don't need your wife to change in order for you to be successful. You, by yourself, can create safeness for yourself, and help her feel safer too. The result will be healthier, more joyous sexual experiences for both of you.

You must look at and eliminate the judgments that impede being sexually open, vulnerable and intimate. Let's begin with your judgments about her body. Do you fully accept her body? What are your *real* thoughts about her fat bulges, her stretch marks, her sagging, off-center, small or large breasts, her hairs on her nipples, her varicose veins, her crooked teeth, her big nose, her imperfect skin, her big or flat butt, or her smell? For your sex life to soar, you must feel completely satisfied with her alluring body, with no thoughts that you are deprived or missing out. When it is, your wish to have lustful thoughts and desires about other women will begin to fade.

How can you tell if you feel sexually safe with your wife? One way is by noticing your sexual thoughts. When you have a sexual thought, is it about her? During my first marriage, I masturbated regularly. My sexual fantasy was *never* about my wife. In fact, I used to wonder if there was something wrong with me, because even when I tried to visualize her as my fantasy partner, I couldn't stay with it. I decided that it must mean I hold her in such high regard that I don't want to imagine living out my sexual fantasies with her. I later realized that this was actually a sign that I did not feel safe with her, for many reasons.

I never once in ten years of marriage revealed to my wife that I masturbated. I felt ashamed of this habit and certain that she would be critical and judgmental of me if she knew. I had "something to hide." My hidden sexual fantasies were a major factor in the ultimate breakdown of our marriage. You need to make sexuality an open, comfortable topic with absolutely nothing to hide from your partner. This will make your sexuality real and safe between the two of you, and not a taboo topic. "Taboo" automatically means "unsafe." Taboo means that each of you have "judgments" about this topic, and therefore avoid it. The path to being real lies in taking the bowl off your lamp. In other words, pro-actively explore the very topics about which you are uncomfortable and have been avoiding.

One such topic is sexual language. I once did an exercise in that personal growth course I took where we intentionally wrote down every "dirty" sexual word we could think of. One woman in my group was an ex-prostitute. She added many words I had never heard of. Do you know there is even a crude word for a vaginal fart? I didn't even know there was such a thing as a vaginal fart! In speaking and writing down these words, we began to look at the judgments we had about these words. We all agreed that the nastiest word was the one for the female genitals. We took turns saying this word out loud. Our goal was to get rid of our judgments about it. When I said it, I could feel the hateful, cut-to-the-heart condemnation wrapped in my tone of voice. For me, that word was the ultimate insult, intended to cut down a person like a knife to the throat. Then we tried saying this same word lovingly, eyeball to eyeball with a classmate. The "power" of this word began to dissipate for me. I began to see that it is a word like any other word, and that its evil, judgmental nature was anchored in my judgmental intentions, not in the word itself.

The truth of this comes home when you learn about curse words in other languages. In French-speaking Canada, three of the nastiest swear words are these: Host. Tabernacle. Chalice. As an English-speaking person, how offended do you feel right now by these words? They are nothing! But when I learned to speak French and acquired the judgmental attitude that goes behind these words, believe me, they have power!

Ridding myself of my judgments about sexual, vulgar words has allowed me to be very comfortable about using these words with my wife in the privacy of our bedroom. The result is sparks and fireworks of the best kind. Great sex requires the paradoxical ability to safely go to a dangerous place. Speaking sexually "taboo" words in a loving, playful way with each other draws you into each other, allowing you to become one flesh, not just in body but in heart and spirit too.

If your partner doesn't fulfill your every sexual fantasy, then you need to explore this unmet need of yours somewhere safely. Suppressing your truth is hypocritical and not real. Furthermore, hiding your truth will only lead to emotional distance, unsafeness between the two of you, and the very real danger that when Satan lays temptation in your path, you will falter.

The key to overcoming this risk is to look at your fantasies and reach a place of peace with them. Your fantasies are anchored in judgments. You are seeing your present situation, comparing it to your fantasy and deciding that the fantasy is better. The proof of this is that you are even having a fantasy! If you had no fantasy, you would have nothing to compare your reality to, and you would automatically be thankful in all things, as the Bible tells us. Being thankful and present-moment focused is one of the great rewards that come to those who are non-judgmental.

What are some common fantasies for men? One is of the sexual woman who desires you and your body above all. Not only is her body sexually perfect, she performs every sexual act your lustful heart desires. She wants sex anytime, anywhere, and in the most dangerous places: at the office, in the car, and in the kitchen. She enjoys sex in every imaginable position. I know for me, I replayed these fantasies over and over again, usually with some "fantasy" woman from my past, or with the help of pornographic materials.

When I became a believer, God healed many of these desires for me. I immediately threw away my pornographic videos and magazines. The scales fell from my eyes and I saw for the first time that I truly had seen women as sex objects for all of my life up to that point. I admitted to myself that the real me often scanned a woman's body, noticing her sexuality. I admitted to myself that I had derogatory thoughts about women if I felt threatened, in sharp contrast to my nice self-image as a "modern" man who supported women's rights and career advancement. When I was born again in Christ, God revealed the "real" me to myself, and changed my heart. Suddenly I saw women as my sisters in Christ. What a gift that was!

However, lust doesn't end that easily. Ridding yourself of your sexual fantasies is nearly every man's struggle, especially a believing Christian man who *wants* to follow Christ's teachings. You must get rid of the fantasy, and the way to do that is to get rid of your judgments about sexuality. You must focus on this one question over and over again, "How do I accept this?" How do you accept her body and her sexual preferences so that you are completely at peace about these? You will know you have succeeded if you have no thoughts about these former fantasies. When you succeed, you will find that you have created a safe emotional space for your wife, thereby *increasing* her ability to willingly explore becoming the full sexual creature God intended her to be too!

In this same spirit of acceptance, you must stop judging your own body. If you are judgmental about your body in any way, this will inhibit your sexuality. How do you feel about the size of your penis, the shape of your stomach, your impotency or sterility, the hair or lack of hair on your chest, and so on? How do you feel about the length of time you can sexually perform, your loss of an erection right in the heat of the moment, or your ability to help your wife achieve orgasm? Judgments about these issues will dampen your sexuality and your connection with your wife, and lower your own self-esteem. When you learn to be non-judgmental, you accept that God created you perfectly as you are, and that there is nothing to hide or be ashamed about.

The ultimate challenge for any man is to arrive at a state of peace with the sexual desires that will never be met. Your first line of defense is to trust in the Lord that because you are having the thought doesn't mean you will act on it. Failing that, you must intentionally and pro-actively grieve the loss of your fantasies. Fantasies and dreams are what motivate us, not just in sex but also in life. Though they are not real, they *seem* real in our minds. We must dig them out, see them for what they are, and grieve their loss. A support group is the best place to do this, rather than with your wife. If your wife is incredibly centered and secure in her sexuality, perhaps you can express your fantasies to her, and if she doesn't take your losses personally, she will be able to listen, empathize and be compassionate about your loss. Not many women can do this, any more than you can do the same for her. The next chapter will focus on what it takes to rise to that level of compassion in a non-judgmental way.

Group Study: Real Lesson 2-6: What conversation about sex do you need to have with someone you love? Perhaps it is your spouse. What are you hiding from her or him? How do you feel about speaking your truth? Perhaps it is your pre-teen or teenager. What judgments about sex are holding you back? Do you feel embarrassed? What is embarrassing about this topic for you? Are you inadvertently allowing their friends to be their sex educators? What do you think your silence is communicating to them about sex as a safe or unsafe topic with you?

NOTES

Lesson 3

YOU ARE COMPASSIONATE, NOT RIGHTEOUS

While playing baseball, my young son taught me the truth of what it means to be compassionate, not righteous. We were in our backyard. Jared was six years old and just learning how to bat the ball. I pitched the ball to him gently and accurately down the middle of the strike zone. His bright blue eyes focused intently on the ball, and with a mighty swing, he missed! I pitched again. He missed again. I pitched again. He missed again! His frustration began to show on his face, as he let out a couple of "aw's!" Finally, after missing six pitches in a row, his frustration poured out.

"Da-a-ad! You're throwing the ball too high!"

I took a quick breath. *I'm pitching the ball too high?* I was caught completely off-guard. I thought, *I'm not pitching too high! You're just missing the ball and blaming me for it!* I checked myself, however. Instead, I focused on being compassionate. I did this by first *mirroring* back his words to him.

"You think I'm pitching the ball too high, do you?" I said casually.

"Yeah! Quit doing that, will ya Dad? I'm never gonna hit the ball if you keep pitching the ball too high!"

I could feel that familiar twinge inside myself as his blame triggered my ego. *Silly kid*, I thought. *He actually thinks the pitcher is supposed to hit his bat, rather than him moving his bat to hit the ball. How am I going to get him to see the obvious?* I wondered.

I decided to focus on being empathetic—seeing the world through his eyes, and not trying to convince him to see the world the way I do. This leadership technique was something that I was constantly trying to improve in myself.

"That ball *is* higher than your bat, isn't it Jared?" I said with some feeling. Then my eyes were opened. He was right! The ball *is* higher than his bat. From his point of view, I was pitching the ball higher than he was swinging the bat. From my point of view, of course, he was swinging the bat lower than the ball. We were *both* right—two opposing truths existing in the same moment in time.

Both of us were justified in blaming the other for not successfully achieving our goal, which was to put the ball into outfield. However, my ability to see his version of the "truth" only happened when I was able to set aside my own righteous version of the truth.

The purpose of this chapter is to learn how to stay centered and at peace when your loved ones blame you for their unhappiness. Your job as a spiritual leader in their life is to help them get over their hurts, disappointments and past wounds. You will help them with this when you embrace Paul's words of wisdom, "You, therefore, have no excuse, you who pass judgment on someone else, for at whatever point you judge the other, you are condemning yourself, because you who pass judgment do the same things" (RO 2:1 NIV) When my son blamed me for failing to hit the ball, it bothered me because I *also* like to blame other people when I am failing! You will readily communicate your compassion for your loved one's difficult situation when you know they are only doing what you yourself have done or could do if you were in their shoes. I expressed this in Lesson 2-2 as *All I See is Me.*

You cannot have compassion for another person if you think their issues are "all about you." When you see that their pain isn't your fault, you will be able to see the world through the eyes of your loved one. This awesome spiritual gift comes to those who can resist the judgmental desire to fix, change, alter or improve the experiences of others. Instead, your compassionate response alone will positively, intentionally and helpfully influence your loved one to see and respond to their situation differently, out of their own free will—or not at all!

Compassion means to "suffer with." When you can simply suffer with someone else, you will experience the tremendous, almost miraculous impact that this kind of love has on those you touch. Compassion is the highest and most difficult form of leadership that I teach in my leadership coaching work, yet is often naively dismissed as easy. Compassion reveals itself as a communication skill, but in reality, it is a skill of the heart. To feel compassion towards another person requires you to have an open, vulnerable heart. Jesus said, "But the things that come out of the mouth come from the heart, and they defile. For from the heart come evil thoughts, murder, adultery, unchastity, theft, false witness, blasphemy." (MT 15:18-19 NAB). You must change your heart to change the words that you communicate with your mouth.

Being compassionate means not only *seeing* the world through the eyes of your loved ones, but also *feeling* it. It is of critical importance that you feel *empathy* for their suffering, and not merely *sympathy*. In the parable of the Good Samaritan, we see this difference. Jesus said, "and when he saw him, he took pity on him." (LK 10:25-37 NIV) The Samaritan's heart was touched and he went on to help the beaten man until he recovered. At no time did the Samaritan attempt to find the robbers or right the wrong that had been done to the traveler. That would have been sympathy. Empathy focuses on the pain of the present moment. Unlike the traveler, your loved ones' injuries are most likely to be emotional, not physical. Your role as a compassionate leader is to help loved ones get over their pain by supportively loving them *during* their pain. This will come easily for you when you understand and believe that *their* pain is not *your* pain. Then, you will be able to stay in the presence of their pain without avoiding them or "fixing" them. The effect on them is that they will often decide to make changes of their own free will.

Righteousness gets in the way of compassion. Not because a righteous person cannot feel compassion, but rather because our desire to be righteous makes it difficult to *be* compassionate. We get derailed by righteousness because it leads us to want to fix, change, alter or improve the other person's experience so that they will be "better" according to our definition. This, in itself, is a judgment. Righteousness can cause us to want to prove that we are right, thereby hindering our ability to be compassionate. Compassion requires us to lead others as if we have *nothing to prove*. With nothing to prove, we are able set aside our own need to rescue, give answers and fix problems. This leaves us feeling compassionate towards their needs, suffering with them just as Jesus suffered for us, and takes on our suffering even now.

A compassionate person may *completely disagree* with the views of another, and yet he is able to walk in the shoes of the suffering of the other, no matter how self-inflicted or misguided he or she may be. Paul wrote, "Do not let any unwholesome talk come out of your mouths, but only according to their needs, that it may benefit those who listen." (EPH 4:29 NIV) Compassion means being able to give other people what they need to hear, not what you need to tell them. This will come readily, for you when you know that their pain is not about you.

The following two stories about caring for elderly people with Alzheimer's Disease demonstrate the impact of compassionate empathy when facing another person's emotional pain.

3-1. Stopping Emotional Outbursts: Alzheimers

He could hear rattling sounds coming from the kitchen, metal scraping against metal. "What is she up to this time?" he asked himself in exasperation. He grunted as he lifted his weary seventy-five year old body out of the armchair, leaving behind the suspenseful closing moments of *The Price is Right* flickering brightly on the television. He stepped into the kitchen to see her standing over the sink holding two metal stovetop element underpans. He glanced over at the two holes gaping out from the stove top.

"What are you doing?" he asked evenly.

"What do you mean, what am I doing?" she snapped. "Can't you see? This is a dirty mess. I've got to get these clean." She began scrubbing harder.

"Let me help you," he offered. He gently took the element protectors from her and began patiently scrubbing. They were surprisingly dirty, he had to admit. As he finished up, he looked over at the remaining two protectors sitting under the stove top elements. "We might as well do these two as well, eh?" he mused.

As he lifted out the elements and removed the protectors from underneath the elements, she took one look at them and grew visibly upset. "These are filthy!" she exclaimed. "They will never get clean. We've got to just throw them out and get new ones."

He could feel his temperature begin to rise. "We can't just throw them out," he protested. "You've got to *order* new ones first, and until then, we *need* these ones."

He took a deep breath. Every day had become an adventure with this woman he'd lived with and loved for fifty years. Alzheimer's Disease had changed her so much, and his life along with it. His mind briefly flashed back to easier times, when he ran the farm and she ran the house and kids. Now he was a "caregiver," a role he had dutifully accepted four years earlier when she was first diagnosed. He had vowed to his adult children, "She looked after me my whole life, and now I'm going to do the same for her for as long as I can."

Suddenly, she burst out, "I am NOT using these filthy things ever again!" She was furious. "This has to go into the garbage. Right now!" With that, she grabbed the dirty stove pan and stormed out of the kitchen, through the family room, and into the back yard. Oblivious to the winter cold, she marched straight to the back of their deep backyard, limping from the pain in her left hip. He hurried after her, shouting, "Hey, what are you doing? Wait a minute, will ya?"

She paid no attention to him. Once near the back, she stopped, planted both feet, and hurled the pan as hard as she could against the back fence, where a compost pile lay steaming. He instantly felt that familiar boiling blood feeling coming on. He felt it nearly every time she had one of these emotional blowouts. He knew that he had to fight that feeling as much as he could. This was one of those times, however, when she was pushing him past his limits.

As he caught up with her, he carefully measured his words to keep his cool. "I guess I just can't handle it anymore," he said to her. "If you won't make it easier on me, then I guess we're going to have to..." he paused for effect, "...put you in a home, where someone else who is better than me can look after you."

She instantly calmed down, responding meekly, "I don't want to go into a home. You do a good job for me. I know I can't get by without you." He went over, picked up the element protector. They began walking towards the house. "Whew!" he thought with relief and some satisfaction. "That settled her down in a hurry."

This man's leadership goal was to get his wife to *stop* her emotional outburst and erratic behavior. And he succeeded! The question is, did he do it with compassion? Her greatest fear was to be put into a nursing home. He knew this, and when her emotions went out of control, he couldn't take it anymore. He used "the hammer" to scare her into changing her behavior. That is what judgments are designed to do—scare people into changing to meet your own needs. When he played the "nursing home card," he triggered one of his wife's deepest fears.

We can guess what made it difficult for him to be compassionate. He had a "right" answer about the stove underpans. New ones needed to be ordered first. In a small but significant way, he had something to prove—that you don't throw old underpans out before you get new ones! Having expertise about a particular subject is often the biggest barrier for a person trying to show compassion to another person. The "expert" trying to show compassion also wants to prove he or she has the right answer. But what the other person needs is not your opinion or advice. The other person needs your love and compassion.

Are you able to feel compassion for the man in this story? Being a caregiver of an Alzheimer's patient is one of the most demanding roles any human being can undertake. It is a disease in which its sufferers replay deep, unresolved emotional hurts from the past. Its sufferers are irrational, illogical, and temperamental. The man in the story is doing the best he can with what he knows, and within his limits. So are you.

In this next story, you will see how an expert caregiver uses non-judgment to compassionately initiate a major turnaround in an Alzheimer patient's behavior.

Naomi Feil is the author of a remarkable book for Alzheimer's caregivers called *The Validation Breakthrough*, which describes a technique that she calls Validation Therapy. She has developed this process during more than forty years of work with the aged, and it is now used in over ten thousand agencies worldwide. Simply stated, Validation Therapy is a form of compassionate empathy. In her experience, by validating an Alzheimer's patient's feelings three times a day for just five minutes at a time, no patient over the age of seventy ever progresses to the debilitating "vegetative" state of Alzheimer's Disease. That is truly a miracle of love! Such is the power of compassion when you empathize with another person. You can learn more about Naomi's life-changing work at www.vfvalidation.org.

Empathy is a leadership skill that has one main benefit: it helps another person get over his or her emotional pain. Because life is full of losses, your ability to help your loved ones grieve their losses is one of the most powerful and frequently used skills you can have in your leadership tool bag. Empathy works anytime, whether your loved one is feeling a major loss like injury and death or a minor loss like the daily disappointments of a burnt dinner or a scraped knee.

The challenge of being empathetic in the face of your loved ones' emotional distress is highlighted in this story from Naomi Feil's book, *The Validation Breakthrough*.[2] Naomi describes an experience where, as an expert caregiver, she felt she should know how to validate a person's feelings in any circumstance. In this abbreviated version of her story, Naomi tells a story in which even her prodigious skills were challenged beyond the edge of her limits.

---

2 Feil, Naomi, *The Validation Breakthrough* (Health Professions Press 1993), 149–155. Used with the author's permission.

Eighty-five year old Lucy Kelly was a former department store buyer, a very unhappy person suffering from Alzheimer's Disease. One day, Naomi walked in to Lucy's room. Lucy greeted her with a scowl. "Get the hell out of my room! Bitch." Patiently, Naomi reasoned with her. "Now, Mrs. Kelly, my job is to make you feel better." Lucy responded by mimicking her in a sarcastic tone of voice, "I don't want to feel better, so you better find another job. I don't talk to idiots."

Naomi responded feebly. "I like my job and I like you. I want to help you."

"LIAR!" shrieked Lucy.

Naomi stared at her in shock, then quietly said good bye and went out into the hall where she began to cry. She realized that Lucy spoke the truth. Naomi *didn't* like her, with her beady brown eyes filled with hate, and her swollen, puffy cheeks.

You cannot give compassion to someone you dislike, because dislike is a judgment in itself. Furthermore, offering empathy to someone who is directly attacking you is the most difficult, demanding skill of all. Naomi's experience highlights a truth that I have experienced many times myself. Compassionate empathy only works if it is *real*. You cannot hide your judgments. Faking it, as Naomi tried to do, does not cut it. Alzheimer's patients have razor sharp emotional antennae that pick up even the slightest nuance of judgment or falseness in your tone of voice. This makes caregiving them a magnificent way to master the skill of non-judgmental empathy.

Naomi gave Lucy a second try on another day. She tried to be compassionate by guessing how Lucy was feeling, hoping to open her up. She said, "I know how you feel Mrs. Kelly. You were an active woman. Now, you can't even walk. You've lost your wonderful job, your husband and your friends. People looked up to you. You were the life of the party. No wonder you're angry at the world. I would feel angry too."

Lucy spat back. "Oh shut up you fool! I don't care how you feel. You can jump out the window as far as I care. AND DON'T TELL ME HOW I FEEL. I AM NOT ANGRY. NOW GET THE HELL OUT OF MY ROOM BEFORE I CALL SOMEONE TO DRAG YOU OUT. DON'T YOU KNOW WHEN YOU'RE NOT WANTED?"

Guessing at how another adult feels is showing neither compassion nor empathy. It is threatening, especially if you are very close to a truth they prefer to hide and deny. A key aspect of being non-judgmentally compassionate is to accept people exactly where they are, without trying to fix, change, alter or improve them. Otherwise, you are playing God, no matter how well intentioned you are. Breaking this habit will help you simply be present with the pain they are actually expressing.

Later in the story, Naomi describes how she finally cracked the hard outer shell that Lucy kept up to prevent anyone from penetrating her soft, vulnerable, emotionally real self. Naomi spent time getting to know about Lucy, and asking her fifty-four year old daughter about her mother and her life. She began to see the world through Lucy's eyes—an active, commanding woman who had lost her career, her husband and the use of her legs. Her own heart began to warm to Lucy and she found a way to accept Lucy's need to be angry, mean and cold. One day, she again walked into Lucy's room.

"Good morning, Mrs. Kelly," she sang cheerily.

"Oh shut up. What's good about it?" Lucy's voice sounded dull and flat.

Naomi echoed her tone of voice, and mirroring her words back to her. "Are you saying there is nothing good about the morning?"

"That's right. You said it," Lucy answered. "That's the way it is. No more. No less. So why don't you leave me alone. Scat!" However, her tone of voice suggested she only half-meant her words.

Naomi continued rephrasing. "With nothing to do, there's no use in talking?"

"You said it!" Lucy responded, looking Naomi in the eye for the very first time. This was the moment of compassion that changed everything. Naomi accepted Lucy's view of the world without judging it. Her ready acceptance of Lucy's view created safeness for Lucy. Lucy finally opened up, freely and willingly. Naomi built on this by beginning to ask non-judgmental questions designed to understand Lucy without trying to fix, change or alter her. She asked Lucy, "Mrs. Kelly, what does a buyer in a big department story do?"

Later, Lucy's fifty-four year old daughter learned this same technique, once she softened her own heart towards her mean, spiteful mother. One day she said, "I know you hate it here, Mother, but there's nothing I can do."

"If you cared, you'd do something. You don't care!" This is a classic example of a loved one using judgments to guilt and shame us into doing what they want. Fortunately, her daughter accepted that without feeling judged.

"Mother," she responded, "you think that if I cared, I would take you out of here?"

"That's right. I'm a burden to you. You don't want me around."

Again, her daughter rephrased. "You think that nobody wants to be with you because you can't walk or work?"

"That's exactly what I think. Without my legs and my job, I might as well be dead." Lucy began to sob. Her daughter no longer tried to calm her down. She stayed with her pain, validating her feelings without judgment. Day by day, they rebuilt their relationship.

Offering empathy when under attack is a demanding task. Jesus was often under attack for his claims, his miracles, and his bold rejection of the legalistic teachings and hypocritical practices of the Jewish high priests. In one example, Jesus demonstrated compassion in response to his attackers: **"Again the Jews picked up stones to stone him, but Jesus said to them, "I have shown you many great miracles from the Father. For which of these do you stone me?"** (JN. **10:29-32** NIV). Asking nonjudgmentally why you are being attacked is one way to gather information so you can feel empathy for the other person's judgments and attacks. In this case, Jesus heard their answer (blasphemy), and then asserted himself, explaining why they were mistaken. When they rejected his answer, **"they tried to seize him, but he escaped their grasp."** (JN **10:39** NIV) He made no attempt to punish them (the hammer), nor did he agree with them by denying His own truth (the doormat). Communicating your compassion to others is not complicated. It is, however, a challenge!

Group Study: Compassion Lesson 3-1: Practice these two steps to effective listening, using any topic.

1. Mirror their words. Reflect back their exact words. For example, he says, "I found a new job!" You say, "You found a new job, did you?" This powerful technique validates that you've heard their words.
2. Empathize with how they feel. Ask them, if they don't express it. "How do you feel about that?" When they express it, empathize using statements like, "I can imagine I might be nervous too, if I were you." Remember, you are not agreeing with them. You are communicating that you understand how *they* feel.

NOTES

_____

_____

_____

_____

_____

3-2 Helping Them Get Over It: Your reputation for being late

It is very difficult to feel compassion towards someone who is judgmental about your habits, mannerisms and preferences. In this next story, we see how difficult this can be, and what you can do about it.

_____

The phone rang. Jim looked at the call display. Ah, his friend Sally.

"Hi Sally!" he said brightly.

"Hi Jim," she laughed at his instant recognition of her. "Isn't that Call Display a handy little device?"

"Yeah, it sure is," he replied. They chatted for a bit to catch up. Then she got to the point of her call.

"Jim, can you bring along those trophies from last year's contest? I'm organizing this year's event and I'll be needing them to present to the winners."

"Oh sure," he replied, remembering where he had put them.

"Now, you won't forget them, will you?" she asked with a gentle chiding in her tone of voice.

He felt an instant pang of guilt shoot through his chest. Chuckling a bit to cover up his discomfort, he said, "Are you saying that Sally, because I forgot to return those dishes you left behind here last summer?"

"Well, you did forget them, didn't you?" she said, also chuckling.

"You're right; I did, although twice you showed up at meetings when I wasn't there." He couldn't help defend himself a little bit. "I'll do my best to remember to bring them along this time."

"That would be great," responded Sally cheerfully. "Oh," she added, "and don't be late for the meeting this time either, okay?"

He felt a ping as his mind shot back to their last meeting together. He grimaced as he remembered that he had indeed been five minutes late, holding up the entire meeting and a room full of fifty people. He decided to be authentic. "You don't forget these things easily, do you Sally? What does a guy have to do to get off the hook with you?" He felt at ease being frank with Sally, a woman with whom he'd had many honest conversations over the years of their friendship.

"Easy," she said brightly. "Just show up on time."

"Ha ha," he retorted laconically. Then he ate humble pie. "I will be there on time, my dear, on Thursday at 7:30 at the community center... no I mean, Sunshine Hall!"

"Now, you're really making me nervous!" she said. "Yes. Sunshine Hall. And don't forget, it's next week, not this week. Maybe I should also be telling you that the meeting starts at 7:00 P.M. just to get you there on time!"

"Yeah, maybe you should," Jim replied. "That's one way to make sure I get there!" His patience was wearing a bit thin at her on-going digs about his tardiness. "Sally, I've got to go now. Thank you for the call and I'll see you next week."

In this example, we can expect that Jim is in all likelihood going to appear on time and at the right location for his next meeting with Sally. She certainly made that point loudly and clearly, and he clearly agreed to live up to his commitment this time. Nonetheless, Sally has damaged her relationship with Jim. He sees that if he makes a mistake or errs with her, she will hold it against him in the form of a judgment, wielding his past "sins" as a weapon to shame him so that he doesn't "do it to her" again. Assuming he does show up on time, her judgmental approach to leading him, that is, to get him to show up on time, will have succeeded, and once again her judgmental approach to leadership will have served her purposes. However, it will have come at the price of a damaged relationship.

People have tremendously accurate memories of times when you hurt or disappointed them, even as they themselves seem to have no recall of their own shortcomings. Many people, like Sally in this case, love to use your past mistakes as a way of "condemning" you, by judgmentally pointing it out in the belief that this will correct your wayward behavior.

There are two issues that arise out of this situation. The first challenge is how to not slide into wanting to judge Sally in return. The second challenge is how to influence Sally toward using a different approach in the future. Let's take them one at a time.

The risk you face anytime someone judgmentally points out your faults is that you will want to be judgmental in return. You get triggered like this: "You think I'm stupid? Well, I'm not half as stupid as you are. You can't even figure out how to turn off the VCR!" There is only one way in which you can avoid this trap in the face of pointed yet truthful judgments. **Agree with the other person.** Eat humble pie. Acknowledge that what she is saying is true. Admit your mistake, and go with it *completely*. "Yes, you're right! I did show up late, and that was very thoughtless of me! Remember how the *whole* room was sitting there waiting for me? Golly, the organizers were not too happy about that! I really blew it! I'm amazed they even let me in that night!"

When people are judgmental, they want to punish you. They want you to admit your mistake, express your remorse, and grovel in shame. We have seen numerous examples of this process in American politics. President Bill Clinton and his sexual affair with Monica Lewinsky is an example. While Mr. Clinton admitted his deed was wrong and ultimately showed deep remorse, there were those who wanted more vengeance. When you have nothing to prove, this need diminishes. You let go of your desire for vengeance. "Beloved, do not look for revenge but leave room for the wrath; for it is written, "Vengeance is mine, I will repay, says the Lord." (RO 12:19 NAB)

Judgments feed our ego and artificially inflate our self-worth. We think, "How could they? I'd never do that!" Your capacity for compassion will grow immensely when you accept that you could indeed "do that!" Do you think the military officers who ran the Nazi death camps in World War II ever imagined when they were eighteen years old that twenty years later they would be overseeing the slaughter of millions of Jews? I sincerely doubt it. Satan draws us in, one judgmental moment at a time, convincing us that we are more worthy, better and superior. Jesus pointed out this risk for all righteous men and women in the parable of the Pharisee and the tax collector. The Pharisee prayed about his many good deeds. The tax collector, however, beat his breast and said, "God have mercy on me, a sinner." Of him, Jesus said, "I tell you that this man, rather than the other, went home justified before God. For everyone who exalts himself will be humbled, and he who humbles himself will be exalted." (LK 18:13-14 NIV). To be judgmental is to exalt yourself.

Eating humble pie takes great courage and strength of character. The line-up for humility is a short one. Television evangelist Joyce Meyers once highlighted the truth of this. She said she once produced an audiotape series on humility. Of the many tapes and books she has produced, she said this was her ministry's worst seller. The worst! Our ego fights humility with every fiber of our being. For this reason, I believe the Lord gives us experiences that force us to face our sinful nature. We must surrender our ego-driven desire to righteously defend ourselves, rather than compassionately reach out in love to others.

Group Study: Compassion Lesson 3-2: "There may be an element of truth in what you're saying." Think of the last time you had a disagreement with someone. Was there an element of truth in his or her judgments about you? If you can't see any, can you imagine how the person might see one anyway, even if he or she is misinterpreting or misunderstanding what you said or did? Have someone offer a criticism of you and respond using this phrase. How does it feel to accept the person's judgments of you without argument? Being compassionate includes accepting condemnation that sometimes doesn't belong to you, just as Jesus did for us.

NOTES

3-3 Breaking the Cycle: 12 Judgments That Hurt

Marriage is the ultimate test of your ability to be non-judgmental. God has paired you with someone who knows *exactly* how to please you, and *exactly* how to get under your skin. St. Paul acknowledged, "But those who marry will face many troubles in this life, and I want to spare you this." (1 COR 7:28 NIV) Paul says that if you can serve God without needing to be married, you will do better. Since few of us are that good, we who are married face a difficult challenge!

Men are called to hold their wives as holy and blameless (Eph 5:25). Wives, in turn, also have a difficult job to do according to that same scriptural teaching, which states that they are to "Submit to your husbands as to the Lord." (EPH 5:22 NIV) Paul compares the relationship between a husband and wife to that of Jesus and the church. Jesus holds the church holy and blameless. The church in turn, is submitted to Him. We submit freely and willingly *because* Jesus holds us blameless, in spite of our sins.

These are linked, and for that reason, I believe this teaching is still relevant in today's modern age. If a man holds his wife blameless, she will *want* to follow him, freely and willingly. If he is judgmental, pressuring her to do what he wants, then she will resist. Furthermore, if a man is using Jesus as his role model, he will readily see that Jesus does not "command and control." Neither should a man do so with his wife.

Despite many women's fears that this Biblical passage gives men a "dictatorial" role as head of the household, the role is not one to be envied. Jesus led the church by laying down his life for her. Holding your wife holy and blameless involves the same sacrifice at an emotional and spiritual level. To be non-judgmental about her habits and behaviors is to die for her.

Your spouse is in your life as the most important person to transform you into the spiritually mature leader God wants you to be. As a man, your wife will fulfill this role if you fulfill your spiritual duty. You must learn how to set aside your own needs in order to meet her needs, just as Jesus did for the church. This duty will lead you through an experience of suffering, and you will see that God has prepared a sweet reward for men who willingly do so. You will be asked to give what your wife needs from you *at your own expense*. That is the suffering part. Once you do it, however, you will receive the joyous part. Your relationship with

God and your reliance on Him will *soar* and you will feel increasingly on fire, filled with the grace, love and inner confidence that come from the Holy Spirit.

Here is how to become non-judgmentally compassionate. You decide that, by yourself, you will give her what she needs in your marriage. There will be no, *"I'll change if you change"* or couples therapy. You alone will change. You will not demand any changes from her, though you will make increasingly clear what your boundaries and limits are in your relationship. The effect will be to *sever* your reliance on your wife to meet your love needs, causing you to rely on God alone to fill your need for love from the inside. Paul says in 1 Corinthians 7:29, "What I mean brothers is the time is short. From now on those who have wives should live as if they had none." (NIV) This does not mean that you will be abandoning your wife. It means that you will not *be dependent* on her for your emotional needs. You must *want* her, not *need* her. With this attitude, your ability to be compassionate towards her will increase dramatically. You will be relying instead on God as your source of love, who says, "I will never forsake you or abandon you." (HEB 13:5 NAB)

You will begin by watching for the ways in which *her* judgments trigger *your* judgments. Then you will make it your goal to accept those judgments, so that you will feel at peace if and when she is judgmental towards you. Your goal is to accept her exactly as she is, with no desire to prove to her that she is partly to blame for the state of your marriage.

Below is a list of common judgments that she may use on you and that you on her. You will likely have done every one of these yourself. Your challenge, however, is to notice when she does these to you and to accept these hurtful judgments without wanting to change her.

1. **Unforgiven:** You did something hurtful to her, and she keeps reminding you of how you did it to her. No matter how much you apologize or try to make amends, she won't let it go. She uses your past behavior to justify why she can't or won't give you what you want. For example, you admitted your lustful desire for other women. Maybe you even crossed the line. Often it's much smaller, for example, you criticized her, or didn't do what you said you would do. Now she holds it against you.

   If you feel bad when she does this, it is your evidence that you agree with her. Seek the Lord's forgiveness and know that this is good and sufficient.

2. **False Accusations:** She takes something you said or did and spins it into something you never intended it to be. Then she tells you or others how you "did it to her." For example, you decided to work late, and that got spun into "you don't care about me or the family. All you think about is yourself." A twist on this one is when she forgets what you actually said, and instead accuses you of saying words you never said. For example, you say you don't really like the colors she chose for the bedroom. She later says you think she's a terrible home decorator, words you never said but that she inferred because you didn't support her choice of colors.

   Remember that "terrible home decorator" is her own inner critical voice speaking. Your dislike of her colors has triggered her own self-judgments. Be empathetic in response, just as Naomi Feil was with Lucy in the earlier Alzheimer's story.

3. **Self-destruction:** She doesn't like a decision you've made so she exaggerates whatever you requested in a way that is self-destructive. She intentionally hurts herself as a way to hurt you. This is sometimes called, "biting off your nose to spite your face." For example, you ask her to get a job, so she takes the very first, back-breaking, awful job she can find and blames you for her unhappiness in that job. Another example is that you ask her to call you if her plans change. She then calls you about every little thing, sarcastically telling people how you "keep her on a tight leash." Her goal is to be a victim, with you as the persecutor.

   You need to pray for strength. You're not doing it to her. She's doing it to herself. Own your half of the deal—what you asked for or said. Empathize with her pain. Remind her she is free to make new choices and that you support her. Accept the possibility that you might not like her choices. Can you live with it anyway?

4. **Hypocrisy.** She is critical of something you do, and then later on does the very same thing herself. For example, you forget to keep a promise to do a chore of some kind. Within a few days, she herself forgets to keep a promise she made to you. You can't resist the temptation to point that out to her, resulting in a fight.

   Remember "All I see is me." She is merely doing what you yourself have done. Stay focused on the present moment issue—the broken promise, and what to do about it. Remember what Paul wrote about love: "It keeps no record of wrongs." (1 COR 13:5 NIV)

5. **Sabotage.** She sets you up for failure. She agrees to do something, then turns around and breaks the agreement. For example, you agree to spend money on a major vacation if she will postpone the purchase of a major household item. Once the vacation is over, she changes her mind and wants the item too. If you don't give in, she begins to blame you for her unhappiness, finding fault in anything you say or do in the hope that you will give in.

   This is a boundary battle. You used conditional love, compromising to get what you wanted. Don't compromise. Jesus said, "And if someone wants to sue you and take your tunic, let him have your cloak as well." (MT 5:40 NIV) When you give, don't link it to getting a future benefit. Then you will have nothing about which to feel judgmental.

6. **Undermining.** She sees you enjoying a success of some kind, and expertly finds fault with what you are doing, the way you are doing it, or predicting impending failure if you keep doing it the way you are doing it. Her pessimism knocks you down in a demoralizing way.

   Is there an element of truth in what she is saying? Then agree with that. Do you feel led by the Spirit? If so, rely on that. If not, pray for discernment. It is more important for you to be true to God's will than to have her approval (see Lesson 5, "Be Purposeful").

7. **Derailing.** You are trying to solve issue A, and she diverts the issue off onto side topic B. For example, you are upset about a money matter, and she turns it into a battle about how you never support her career. Or, you want her to listen to your problem and instead, she starts telling you about *her* problem.

   Respond to this by mirroring and empathizing. Be at peace with the knowledge that you are modeling yourself after Jesus, putting her needs ahead of yours. When she feels heard by you, your turn will come. If it never comes, remember that Jesus is your first line of support, and she is second. You already have first prize. Grieve any sense of loss you have that your needs are not being met by her. This will strengthen your reliance on God, not her. Then you will be able to love her exactly as she is, without needing her to be different.

8. **Rigid & stubborn.** You want some compromise from her and she won't give an inch, no matter what approach you take. Perhaps you disagree about an issue regarding renovating the house, where to live, or how to handle a parenting challenge. You feel frustrated and road-blocked.

   Pray for discernment. Jesus had tough "resist" boundaries in two core areas—desecrating the house of God, and being true to God's will for His life. He let people be free to be who they are. If this level of humility is beyond you, have the fight, but fight non-judgmentally. Don't say "you owe me." Don't label her behavior as stubborn, immature or petty. Stick to the present moment issue, no matter what past debts you each think you are owed.

9. **Forgetfulness.** She forgets something important to you, like meeting you somewhere on time. She got caught up doing her own thing. You were left waiting for her, wondering what happened and missing out on what the two of you were planning to do. You will notice this judgmental trigger when you meet someone who keeps forgetting your name.

   Remember how often you forget, and how often you are mistaken. Her forgetfulness may indeed mean that you are not important for her at this time. Don't take it personally or shame her for this. It's not about you.

10. **Crazy-Making.** She asks you to do something. When you do it, you get criticized for doing the very thing she asked you to do. For example, she says she wants some space from you. So you leave her alone for awhile. Time passes and then she gets angry that you are ignoring her so much. You feel like you can't win, getting criticized regardless of which choice you make.

    This is a tough one. She needs to blame you, because if she doesn't blame you, she would have to blame herself. That's the reason you blame her too, so remember that. Empathy is the best response to this one. When you mirror her words back to her, you help her see herself without judging her, or pointing out her behavior. If you can make this habit known between the two of you, you can sometimes catch it right in the moment and say it—IF you do so with laughter and not as a judgmental criticism.

11. **Betrayal.** You open up to her about your real feelings, hopes and fears. She listens supportively. Two days later, she throws your truth back in your face. For example, you admit you're afraid you may have blown a work

opportunity by not calling a key person on time. When your fears come true, she makes a critical comment about your stupidity in not making the crucial phone call when you should have.

This kind of judgment builds walls between couples. You were vulnerable, and she used your vulnerability against you. Agree with her that there is an element of truth to what she's saying. Be real and tell her that you feel hurt by what she said. Accept whatever response you get. Commit to continuing to be vulnerable with her anyway. The apostle Peter wrote this about Jesus, "When they hurled their insults at him, he did not retaliate: when he suffered, he made no threats. Instead he entrusted himself to him who judges justly." (1 PE 2:23 NIV)

12. **Mind-Reading.** When you ask someone to do something, you are always at risk of being judged. You ask someone to help you work on a backyard project, or help you find a new job. If he agrees, he may resent you for "making" him do it. If he refuses, he may resent you for having had the nerve to ask in the first place! Either way, you are being judged because you failed to read his mind. The person resents the fact that you "put" them in an awkward position. This is sometimes described as "protocol." People want you to protect them from having to be real. You will notice this is happening to you if the person suddenly start avoiding you, or makes subtle digs.

The only way to completely avoid this type of judgment is to make yourself very small. Ask nothing and receive nothing. Make yourself independent and invulnerable from all others. Is this what Jesus did? Not even remotely! As you become more non-judgmental, you will accept that you must be salt and light, true to God's purpose for your life. You can't control how other people respond. When you are very "present," however, you will notice their discomfort. Then you can openly and frankly invite them to be real. Your non-judgmental attitude is the most powerful tool you have to make them feel safe and reveal what they are really thinking and feeling.

These twelve examples of common judgmental responses we each give to our loved ones are meant to make one point clear: this is difficult! Nowhere does that difficulty become clearer than when your marriage is on the rocks, or in actual separation. If we get scared in a love relationship, the worst side of us emerges. Our desire to control and judgmentally punish the other person for hurting us grows wildly! Satan is watching with glee, while fear and darkness fall over us.

Each person in a couple can break this cycle by absorbing the judgments they are receiving from their partner. If no one is willing, then I believe the Lord is calling men to be the first, just as Jesus was the first for us as his church. You will be compassionate, not righteous, when you can see the world through her eyes much more deeply. This means going beyond those things you can imagine you yourself having done, and going to areas where you haven't gone. I want to make this as plain for you as I can by later telling you the story of how the Lord taught me the true meaning of non-judgment when my current wife Joanne left me for the first time, just two years into what is a second marriage for both of us.

Group Study: Compassion Lesson 3-3: Walk in another person's shoes. Visit other churches in other denominations. Spend an hour or a day in someone else's world, as a volunteer at a school, at a nursing home, on a help line. See the world through that person's eyes. Listen inquisitively and with curiosity. Can you see how you might feel the way he or she feels if you were in the person's shoes?

NOTES

_____

_____

_____

_____

_____

_____

_____

_____

3-4 Healthy Boundaries: Breaking the Rescuer Habit

One of the most difficult lessons to learn on the path to being non-judgmental is how to break the habit of rescuing other people. There is a fine line between compassion and rescue. Compassion is rooted in empathetically accepting another person's suffering, without trying to fix his or her situation. Rescuing is rooted in righteously deciding you know better than God what this person needs. Jesus did not rescue every person who came along. A Canaanite woman called out to Jesus, begging him to save her daughter from a demon. He responded by completely ignoring her! When pressed, he finally said, "I was sent only to the lost sheep of the house of Israel." She responded, "Please, Lord, for even the dogs eat the scraps that fall from the table of their masters." (MT 15:24,27 NAB) Her incredible faith moved him to compassion, and he then healed her daughter. You may say, "Isn't that actually an example of Jesus rescuing her?" Yes it is. I am not saying we should not be helpful to those in need. I am saying that you must be at peace with not feeling guilty about their pain and struggles. You aren't doing it to them. You don't owe them anything. You are free to help or not help, just as Jesus did.

Jesus did not try to rescue Judas from his betrayal, though he was well aware of the impending betrayal. Instead, he said, "It would be better for him if he had not been born." (MT 26:24 NIV) He made no effort to "fix" Judas or show him the error of his ways. Jesus demonstrated very strong boundaries in order to allow God's will to unfold according to His plan. Your ability to be compassionate towards others will grow dramatically when you no longer feel obliged to fix, solve, alter or improve their situation. This can hurt if you believe you are responsible for their pain. If they also believe this, they will get upset if you *don't* rescue them! Furthermore, giving up rescuing means giving up the ego-addicting boost that you are their hero. Here is a simple example of how a parent often rescues his or her child, rather than acting with true compassion.

Jason came running up to his father, tears streaming down his cheeks, blubbering between gasps of crying and breathing.

"Dad! Bobby isn't playing fair! He keeps hogging the Playstation controller and won't let me have a turn!" Waaah-h-h!! Jason's wail was deep and sorrowful.

This is a typical parenting moment when Dad has a choice: to rescue or to be compassionate. If he decided to rescue, he might begin by collecting evidence, saying, "How long has Bobby been on the Playstation?"

Immediately, Jason started to feel better as he sees Dad getting hooked. "Forty-five minutes!" he replied indignantly.

"Well, that is a long time." Dad marched over to the family room. "Bobby, how long have you been playing this game?" Dad wanted to test both boys for honesty.

"I don't know," he replied without looking up. "For awhile."

"Bobby, I've told you boys to share this game fairly, or I'm going to take it away from both of you! Now, be nice to your little brother!" Dad waited to see what happened next. If Bobby gave in, Dad would leave feeling satisfied. If Bobby didn't give in, he would put more pressure on him to do so.

At this point, it doesn't really matter what Dad does. He's already blown it. He's decided to play judge and jury, intervening in this typical sibling conflict to rescue little Jason from big, bad Bobby.

Here is what a compassionate, non-judgmental response might look like:

Jason runs up to Dad, tears streaming down his cheeks, and blubbering between gasps of crying and breathing. "Dad! Bobby isn't playing fair! He keeps hogging the Playstation controller and won't let me have a turn!" Waaah-h-h!! Jason's wail was deep and sorrowful.

Dad decides to mirror what Jason has said, in a similar tone of voice that Jason is using. "He keeps hogging the Playstation and won't let you have a turn, huh!"

"Yeah, that's right. It's not fair. Just because he's bigger than me doesn't mean he can just hog it all the time!" (This is a typical judgmental "victim" bait, designed to hook you into fixing the problem).

Dad now has a choice. He can keep mirroring Jason's words and feelings. Or he can begin to empathize with those feelings. Let's say he chooses to empathize. In this case, he doesn't need to ask how Jason is feeling. Jason has made that obvious. "Well son, that must feel unfair when he hogs the controller just because he's bigger than you." Dad is accepting Jason's view of the world, without agreeing with it, nor trying to change it. He is supporting Jason's right to feel the way he feels, without judging either of his sons as right or wrong, good or bad.

Already there will likely be an instant change in Jason's demeanor. He might say, "So! Are you going to *make* him share it with me?" How demanding he will be will depend on how deeply Dad has trained his son that playing the victim gets results. If that is your long-term pattern, your loved ones, whether wife, child or family member, will *increase* their victim role to increase the pressure on you to give in and solve their problem for them. This is an example of "the measure you use, will be measured to you." (MT 7:1 NIV) A history of rescuing will lead to much victim-like behavior. If Dad has good boundaries, he might say, "Thank you for telling me about your problem. Is there anything I can do to help you solve your problem?" This has to be genuine and non-judgmental, not said with contempt or sarcasm.

Becoming aware of your own boundaries and those of others, leads to a growing sense of self-trust that you will do what is right, taking a tough stand on what's yours to defend, and accepting the right of others to do the same. This is the foundation for strong, non-judgmental leadership. This model shows what healthy and unhealthy boundaries look like between two people. Put yourself on the left hand side and the other person on the right hand side:

Peach/Watermelon Boundaries Model

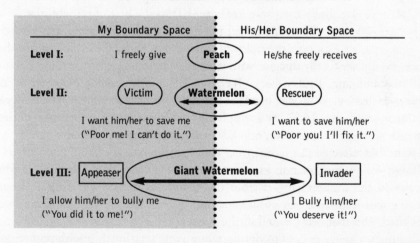

Level I is a healthy, non-judgmental state that I call being a Peach, compassionate on the outside and tough on the inside. Level II is the more common state where people wander in and out of each other's turf with good intentions that are nonetheless anchored in judgmentally-based boundary violations. At this level, people are being ordinary-sized Watermelons. Martha exhibited this when she complained to Jesus that Mary was not helping her with the house work. "Lord, don't you care that my sister has left me to do the work by myself? Tell her to help me!" (LK 10:40 NIV) She is playing victim, trying to lure Jesus into her space and fix her problem. Jesus wisely resisted. Level III involves serious boundary violations that can crush a person's self-esteem as the invader takes control of the appeaser in a deep and violated way, including sexual, emotional and physical abuse. I call this being a Giant Watermelon.

The sin of violating boundaries is captured in the Lord's Prayer when we pray, "Forgive us our trespasses as we forgive those who trespass against us." To trespass is to cross a boundary that isn't ours to cross. The cure is to fervently pray for forgiveness in the same measure with which we forgive others.

On the other hand, the preventative vaccine to these boundary violations is captured in the Steady Hands of Jesus symbol on the cover of this book. The upright left hand symbolizes **Resist**. We must resist people who want to cross into our space, that is, to stop luring them in by playing victim (Level II) and to stop appeasing them when they bully their way in (Level III) to the best of our abilities.

The outreached right hand symbolizes **Support**. We are to support the rights of others to do what they want within their space, even if we totally disagree with what they are doing. We must stop rescuing and stop bullying. Paul wrote, "Therefore let us stop passing judgment on one another. Instead, make up your mind not to put any obstacle or stumbling block in your brother's way." (RO 14:13 NIV) Applying this powerful principle is entirely dependent on getting clear on one key question: *What is your space?*

Jesus' life reflected this basic principle. He supported the freedom of others to willingly follow him, or not. He resisted space He considered His own, as when he chased the moneychangers from the temple to defend His Father's house. Once gone, Jesus took no punitive action against them. His boundaries were defended, and that was the end of the matter.

Boundary space is easy to define when your relationship with someone is quite distant. For example, your neighbor prefers to keep his grass cut high, while you prefer to keep it trimmed short. It's his lawn—he can do what he wants! Emotionally, you are living two hundred feet apart. His decisions about his lawn have no effect on you. It is only when you enter into a closer relationship with someone that boundaries begin to blur. If you don't mind a sink full of dirty dishes and she does, whose space is that? If you want sex three times a week and she wants it once a month, whose space is that? If he wants his family over all the time and you are tired of all this "company," whose space is it?

Importantly, as a parent your boundaries overlap those of your children. At birth, your overlap is 100%. By the age of twenty-one, that overlap should be nearly 0%! Discerning what is your child's boundary and what is yours is the main challenge of being a parent. We learn early on that we can't force certain foods down their throats. But we can control the music they listen to later on. The question is, should we? And to what degree should we? And with what method do we achieve this goal? Non-judgment helps you separate yourself from your child so that you can readily and firmly draw healthy, loving boundaries that have their best interests at heart, not your self-gratification and need for control. This will happen readily when you accept that your sons and daughters belong to God, not you.

To have compassion for someone, you must learn to shrink your boundaries. You must stop being a watermelon. You will know you are a watermelon if you are triggered by what other people do—decisions the government makes, the way your spouse dresses, the eating habits of your children, or what the weather is like. When Joanne left me the first time, I learned just how much of a watermelon I was. I wanted to control her spending, earning, social habits, and children's activities, to name a few big ones. Her behavior triggered me, and I reacted to her choices by being judgmental in order to pressure her to do things my way.

By focusing on accepting the freedom of others to be who they are, the Lord will help you become a peach. Peaches accept that the President of the United States will keep making decisions without even once calling you up to ask your permission or opinion! Peaches accept that God will provide the weather and you will never get a vote on the matter. As a peach, I accept that some men and women will choose to engage in homosexual activity no matter what I say or do. At the same time, Peaches are comfortable about defending their own space and being true to themselves for their own reasons. They resist the attempts of others to lure or pressure them into sinful behavior.

In order to be compassionate, you must accept that life is not fair. In the story of the master who gives three men different amounts of money, Jesus reveals this as truth. He said, "For everyone who has will be given more, and he will have an abundance. Whoever does not have, even what he has will be taken from him." (MT 25:29 NIV) It is not your job to play God, fixing pains that belong to other people—pains that God is allowing in their lives. This doesn't mean that you will become a hard-hearted person. Indeed, being non-judgmental has the opposite effect. As you accept the unfairness of life and your own powerlessness to fix other people, you become aware that your judgments were stopping you from doing something useful in the first place! Your judgments about street bums stopped you from talking to one as you passed by. Your judgments stopped you from giving something to them, as you judgmentally thought they should "go get a job." Jesus did not force salvation on anyone. He gave it freely to those who sought it. Remember that when you are compassionate towards those who are emotionally needy, you are nourishing Jesus himself. "Whatever you did for one of these least brothers of mine, you did for me." (MT 25:4 NAB)

Overall, I believe that if we can love any sinner as Jesus loved the tax collectors, our compassion may help them change their ways. Our challenge is to not be judgmental of them if they don't change, or conversely, judgmental of ourselves for "failing." After all, we are sinners ourselves, and we sin every day. We are in no position to throw a stone at them or anyone else. Nonetheless, you and I must accept that sometimes we will want to judge someone who cuts us off in traffic, treats us disrespectfully, or rejects us. Each time we do, God is giving us one more opportunity to shrink our space, grow more humble, and discern with growing wisdom the best way to respond that will actually get us what we want! When you are non-judgmental, you will discover that you can much more readily influence other people to make real behavior changes. This will be the focus of Lesson Four, titled *You are Wise, not Smart.*

Group Study: Compassion Lesson, 3-4: Become aware of personal boundaries: Identify the boundary level in these exercises. Whose space belongs to whom? Consider what you would do if you responded judgmentally, and then non-judgmentally.

a. **You are on vacation.** A man walks up to you and offers you a free $50 gift certificate for dinner for two if you will spend two hours with him at a breakfast meeting to hear about a fantastic investment opportunity.

b. **Your spouse buys a large yogurt.** Time after time, she buys a large tub of yogurt, only to throw half of it out because it doesn't get eaten fast enough.

This time, you are with her at the grocery store and she reaches out to buy another large tub.

c. **Traffic.** A speeding car pulls up behind you, and sits on your bumper, flashing their headlights at you on a busy multi-lane highway.

d. **You are in a slow line at the check out counter.** You are four back and in a hurry. Suddenly, someone with several items, asks the person at the front to butt in, who agrees without consulting anyone else in the line.

e. **Your seventeen year old child decides to start smoking dope** and having sexual intercourse in your home, behind your back. You discover it by accident.

f. **Dishwasher.** Your spouse criticizes the way you load the dishwasher, nagging regularly at you to rinse every plate and utensil first, before starting up the dishwasher.

NOTES

_____

_____

_____

_____

_____

3-5 Marital Breakdown—The Dilemma of Near and Far

Marriages break down because hope dies. Hope dies because we feel we can never be good enough in the eyes of our life partner. "Not good enough" is the message that you send when you judge your wife or your husband: *"I'm unhappy and it's your fault."* If the judgment ended there, perhaps we could live with that. But it doesn't end there. Like a court of law, a judgment of "Guilty" is followed by the sentencing. This is the punishment designed to "teach" your loved one to never commit that sin again. In marriage, the most popular sentence is emotional distance.

Emotional distance is the measure of the emotional connection that you feel with your spouse. When you first fell in love, before you were married, your connection felt close *and* safe. He farted and she responded with laughter or feigned horror. She complained about her mother and he listened with sympathy. He got drunk and she thought he was hilarious. She spent all her money on clothes and he smiled and told her how gorgeous she looked.

Then you get married. Suddenly, your habits affect each other. His poor hygiene is in her face everyday. Her complaining wears on his nerves like a broken violin. His drinking becomes a serious problem. Her spending drives him crazy. Each of these fuels judgments. Each judgment invites punishment. She gets mad and gives him the cold shoulder for a day, a week or longer. Her distance from him is *Far*. He in turn, gets mad and snarls at her, dark eyes flashing with a menacing look. His distance from her is frighteningly *Near*.

A boundary battle is underway. His hygiene and drinking become her business. Her complaining and spending become his business. Boundaries blur. Two watermelons are overlapping each other's territory and sparks are flying. Emotions get hot and then emotions grow cold. Emotions that are *Near* feel *unsafe*, and you inevitably want to move *Far*. Your relationship becomes like two roommates, sharing the same roof and talking about superficial topics so as to not get too *Near*, lest the sparks begin to fly again. But *Far* also feels unsafe. You don't feel loved. You feel abandoned. Either you or your partner becomes emotionally unavailable and disconnected. You yearn for more—for a return to the love you once felt. As the years go by, your relationship risks falling into what my therapist once described as "shared loneliness." If your commitment to marriage is iron-clad, you may accept that this is all there is. If your pain grows too great, your emptiness may lead one of you to want out of the marriage, hoping to find love again elsewhere.

Emotional distance is a dilemma. If you let her too near, she'll criticize you. So you push her away. Now you are Far. The sparks die down but so does the love. Near feels scary. Far feels scary. At any given moment in time, you can feel the emotional distance in your relationship. Like the weather, emotional distance can change in a heartbeat. My wife once asked me what I thought about the idea of attaching a simple book shelf onto the wall of the boys' bedroom. She showed me how she had emptied the existing bookshelf on the floor and filled it with toys instead. The new bookshelf would be an ideal place to put the newly displaced books! I instantly had a judgmental thought, followed by a comment that was real, not nice! "Why don't you let the boys decide what they want to do with their books instead of you doing it for them?" Her eyes flashed angrily and she said, "Oh, forget it!" and walked out of the room. Our emotional distance went from Near to Far in an instant. I judgmentally disapproved of her desire to arrange the boys' room herself. Her radar instantly picked up the subtle zinger (hammer) contained in my question. Rather than hammering me back, she went into doormat mode. The result was an immediate increase in our emotional distance, from three feet to twenty feet! While the original issue was the book-shelf, in no time flat a new issue surfaced—emotional distance. "She's mad at me." "He's mad at me." We have lost our loved one's approval. We have gained their disapproval instead.

Our relationship with God reveals this same emotional struggle. In the Book of Genesis, Adam and Eve began their relationship with God in a safe, loving and protected way. Then they ate the forbidden fruit. God judged their sin and punished them by putting them out of the Garden of Eden. His love suddenly seemed frighteningly *Far*. He abandoned us. Later in Noah's time, God passed judgment on the people, grew angry and unleashed a great flood, saving only Noah's family and the animals. His fury seems frighteningly *Near*. He judged us as sinners unworthy of living. *Near* feels scary. *Far* feels scary. Either way we are scared. Mercifully, God sent us His only son Jesus to reconcile us to Him. Leaning on Jesus to fill our love needs is the way out of this dilemma. Until we do, we remain stuck in a vicious cycle that appears to have no way out.

The purpose of marriage is to learn one major lesson: we must rely on the Holy Spirit to fill our love needs, and not our husband or wife. Marriage is the perfect place to learn this lesson because in a typical marriage, Near and Far marry each other! Near prefers a good fight about what's bothering him or her rather than sweeping it under the rug. Far prefers silence over a heated argument. Near likes the relationship to be at three feet, having boisterous arguments until his or her hot issue is wrestled to the ground. Far likes the relationship to be at twenty feet, avoiding conflict and smoothing everything over. The Near zone feels like you are always fighting. The Far zone feels like you are never resolving anything. I call this the twenty foot/three foot battle.

God is so wise. He puts Near and Far together because this combination is perfect for your marriage. In the beginning of your love relationship, this combination was perfect! The emotional openness of Near felt exciting to the emotionally disconnected Far. In turn, that very same emotional disconnection felt calm and stable to the volatile and exuberant Near. Near is an attention-seeker. Far is an attention-avoider. These opposite characteristics are highly appealing!

Imagine if it didn't work this way. Imagine if Near married Near, and Far married Far. Near and Near would be like the joke about the guy on a date who spends the whole evening talking about himself. Finally he says, "Enough about me! Let's talk about you. What do you think about me?" Another Near could never tolerate a whole evening with this limelight hog. Far, however, wouldn't mind. At least this way, Far's own habits and quirks are not under scrutiny.

Far and Far, on the other hand, would have conversations that would last about twenty seconds.

"What's happening with you?"

"Nothing much. What's up with you?"

"Nothing really."

"Well... nice talking to you. Have a good day."

Near would never answer "Nothing." Near would tell Far his or her whole life story! Nevertheless, Near and Far are the perfect breeding ground for being judgmental about your love partner. Far partners dislike getting their emotions stirred up and they blame Near for causing them emotional pain by stirring the pot. In turn, Near partners love dealing with their emotions and blame Far for causing them emotional pain by *not* allowing their emotional pot to get stirred! Each person wants his or her partner to fix their pain. Neither is taking owner-ship of his or her own feelings. Far pushes Near away to the twenty foot zone to keep things calm. Near drags Far in to the three foot zone to resolve unhappy issues. It is no more possible to be Near and Far at the same point in time than it is to have the stars shining at high noon! You are causing each other emotional pain by the very nature of your being! You are like oil and water. Someone has to give in or you will break apart!

I believe this is the reason why God did not give a man and a woman an easy way out of a marriage. Jesus said, "But from the beginning of creation, God made them male and female. For this reason 'a man shall leave his father and mother (and be joined to his wife), and the two shall become one flesh.' So they are no longer two but one flesh. Therefore what God has joined together, no human being must separate." (MK 10:6-9, NAB) For those of us who have been divorced and remarried, we have discovered the truth of Jesus' teaching in a particular way. By fencing us in, the Lord is forcing us to find a way to break this deadlock. The emotional dilemma of Near and Far that I failed to resolve in my first marriage was waiting for me in my second marriage. There was no escape. The Lord taught me this lesson in a most painful way when my second marriage fell apart for the first time.

After dating for nearly two years, Joanne and I took the courageous step of getting remarried in the middle of life. Her three children were aged ten, eight and six, while my son was four years old. I was going through a career change and so was she, after being a stay-at-home mother for several years. Both of us had done a fair bit of work on healing our past. We felt ready. Were we ever wrong!

No amount of dating can prepare you for sharing the same roof. Boundaries merge and life becomes a blur. Unlike a first marriage, we instantly had four kids and two ex-spouses who had a significant role in our lives on account of the children and on-going financial commitments. Furthermore, we each felt we had been run over in our first marriages. We were determined not to let that happen again. Instead of generosity, we were prepared to dig in this time around. Near and Far emerged almost the day after we got married!

On our honeymoon, for example, we went to the Grand Canyon. As we prepared to leave the Canyon and head north to Colorado, we sat in our rented car. She was looking at a map. I waited impatiently for her to give me directions. She struggled with it. Finally, I snapped at her, "Give me the darn map!" She looked with shock at me. "*Who is this angry guy?*" she thought, resentfully handing it over to me. My frustrated remark bothered her and she grew distant. I noticed her distance right away and it bothered me. The emotional distance struggle had begun.

Over the next two years, a variety of issues surfaced in our new life together. In every situation, my approach was the same. I wanted to hash out each issue at the three foot mark. I was a classic Near person. She in turn, felt threatened by my close attention to the issues in our lives. She wanted me to back off. She began avoiding talking to me about the real issues in our life. She was a classic Far person at the twenty foot level. As she grew more distant, I grew angrier. As I grew angrier, she grew more distant. The vicious cycle of Near and Far was in high gear! I wanted her to deal with my unhappiness about our issues. She wanted me to move further away, avoiding these intense talks. She said I was crushing her and threatened to leave me. I said she was scaring me and resolved not to let her threats lead to sweeping our problems under the carpet.

This vortex of doom spun ever deeper. Twice I loudly slammed my hand in anger when she wouldn't deal with issues I wanted dealt with. She in turn threatened to leave the marriage. Our judgmental threats grew nearer and further all at once as we fruitlessly tried to get the other person to meet our needs. We felt a growing despair that seemed unstoppably destined to destroy our marriage.

After nearly two years of this back and forth emotional see-saw, we were both at the end of our rope. One day, shortly after she completed an exhausting one year teacher's degree, I got angry with her distance and said she should just move out as she wasn't really in the marriage anyway. "In my opinion," I said, "We are at a hundred feet, not twenty feet! We have a 'roommate' relationship, not a real marriage." With that, she stood up and walked out the door. A few hours later, she called to say she wasn't coming back.

I was shocked. Despite my words, I didn't really mean what I said. That's what happens with the Near and Far dilemma. You use fear to scare the other person into doing what you want. Near scares Far by looking like a Hammer. Far scares Near by acting like a Doormat, passively resisting and avoiding. I could see it happening but I didn't know what to do about it. Over the next six weeks, the Lord revealed the answer to me. I had to move from three feet to twenty feet. I had to stop needing her to be at three feet to assuage my pain. I needed to lean on Jesus and the power of the Holy Spirit to do that.

I love my wife Joanne. She is my dream woman for many reasons, including her love of children, her playful nature, our sexual connection, her love and acceptance of my family, and her love of my upside down sense of humor. She was a happy person while we dated. I felt committed to her and I was certainly committed to the vows I made to her before God. I wanted to do everything in my power to save our marriage. I wanted to keep my eye on the ball—*to win her back*, not to prove she was wrong for leaving, or that she didn't deserve a swell guy like me anyway.

I knew that the first important thing I had to do was Lesson 1: *Accept* her freedom to leave. I knew from my past divorce experience what *not* to do to further scare her off. I did not take legal action, change door locks, or close off bank accounts. I remembered how my first wife had done that and how I had used those responses to confirm to myself that she also wanted the marriage to end—a kind of self-fulfilling prophecy. I also recognized that my Near nature was *causing* her to run away. I had to instantly and completely end that vicious cycle. I did so by not calling her—period. I decided that she had to call me. If she wouldn't call, then so be it. I would have to accept that. This was agonizingly painful for a Near guy like me. Three to four days went by at a time. I found ways to give myself support from within, or I would have broken down and called her for sure. I prayed for strength, asking the Lord what lesson He was trying to teach me. I also wrote constantly in my journal, analyzing our relationship in great detail. I took comfort in Paul's words,"No trial has come to you but what is human. God is faithful and will not let you be tried beyond your strength; but with the trial he will also provide a way out, so that you may be able to bear it." (1 COR 10:13 NAB)

Eventually, she did call. Small talk led to bigger talks. I realized with a broken heart that Joanne sounded exactly the same as I did when I left my first wife. She said I was controlling, rigid and unwilling to give her room to be who she is. She gave me specific examples, such as how I refused to build a wall around my office, leaving myself and my desk intruding wide open into our main living area. I realized I had been ungenerous and unkind. I realized once again how true it is that *All I See Is Me*, just as Paul wrote in Romans 2:1. I would never have believed I could do to her what I myself had so disliked in my first marriage if I hadn't seen it with my own repentant eyes. Lesson 2 was driven home to me—the real me used the hammer with her many times, not listening to her needs, while remaining selfishly focused on me and my needs.

Of course, I could justify every sin I had committed. I tried to convince her that being angry once a month or even once a week was not that much, pointing out examples from other couples we knew. She disagreed. She felt being angry even once was once too often. While I firmly believed there was a ping-pong in our relationship, she resisted. I decided to take the lead and own my wrongs. I wanted her to know that I was a changed man. I apologized sincerely, on bended knee, for the wrongs I had committee in her eyes, listing them off frankly and sorrowfully. She was touched and moved... but not convinced! Her level of fear and distrust was still very high. Somehow, we had to rebuild the trust in our relationship.

I sought professional help from my therapist. He suggested I invite Joanne to come along once, to witness my session with him without asking anything from her.

I wanted her to see the real me, without any pressure on her. She graciously agreed to come along. Being vulnerable like that helped us both. My therapist asked me why I could be openly angry with her but not with other people. He helped me see that there was only one reason—I give myself permission. "Don't give yourself permission!" he wisely advised. My anger stopped that day, permanently.

Even so, I was still making one huge mistake. *I wanted her to return the favor!* I wanted her to acknowledge the wrongs she had done by being Far. I wanted her to share in the blame. She readily agreed that she was wrong to threaten to leave, acknowledging that this was like having a loaded gun on the table. However, she was unwilling to sit with me while I self-righteously justified my behavior by citing all of her faults and weaknesses.

That was the moment the Lord had me where He wanted me—to learn the true meaning of Lesson 3: be compassionate. I had to accept that I had done what I had done without justifying myself. For the first time, I truly understood what it meant to take responsibility for my own actions. Not only must I take the hit for my half of the deal, I had to let her off the hook for my opinion about her half of the deal. The way out of the twenty foot/three foot dilemma was to accept that my three foot nature was wrong, and furthermore, that she was blameless for hanging out at the twenty foot mark! This is the exact opposite of what our sinful nature cries out to do. We want to blame our loved one, while justifying ourselves as innocent victims who were "forced" to do what we did! In the ping-pong game of being judgmental, we want to point out their ping and minimize our own pong. That is not, however, what God wants.

I looked at my list of things I wanted her to address. It was a long list. Could I accept every one of her faults? I felt overwhelmed at the thought. I cried out in my journal, *"Is that it Lord? Do I have to surrender 100%? Is 99% not good enough?"* The hurt in my heart was a suffering and despair deeper than I had ever felt in my life. The Lord's answer vibrated in my heart. *Yes, 100% surrender. Nothing less will do.*

I began to explore surrender. Not only must I be non-judgmental about her decision to leave me, but I needed to actually *support* her need to be Far, including her decision to leave. This was a 180 degree shift from my normal, Near-oriented mindset. I had to not only put my gear shift into neutral by not judging her—I had to shift into gear in the *opposite* direction!

In the sixth week of our separation, Joanne unexpectedly came by with the children. She needed some stuff from the basement. While the kids played, she and I went into the basement. I felt a sudden peace descend over me. I was ready to let her go.

"Joanne, I think the time has come for you to make a decision," I said quietly. "The children have been living in limbo for six weeks, and this uncertainty has become a heavy burden for me. I love you and I want you to come back. But if you feel you must leave, I will support you, whatever you decide. I'll help you get a place to live, give you money as best as I can and do whatever it takes to get you and the kids settled." She looked back at me with soft eyes. "Thank you. I agree. It has been a long time. I will think about it and I will let you know." We hugged and went back to the kids.

Two days later, she called to ask me to join her and the kids at the lakefront in our town. I declined. The previous day I had taken off my wedding ring for the first time. I was done. She called again later that night, saying she wanted to meet with me to talk. I reluctantly agreed. There she told me she wanted to come back. My heart leaped with joy, though it was a changed heart. I knew that I no longer needed her to be at three feet for me to feel loved. I had found a new level of spiritual love in the peace of Jesus Christ even at the twenty foot level.

If you are facing intense conflicts or a chilly distance in your marriage or in other personal relationships, thank the Lord for His gift hidden in your loved one. It is our sinful nature to withdraw our love in order to punish those we love. We do it by getting angry or by getting distant. Near and Far are both forms of emotional abandonment. You will not feel abandoned or attacked if you can accept that they are not doing it to you—they are doing it to themselves! When I am angry at her, I am angry at me. When I am distant from her, I am distant from me. My judgments boomerang right back at me, in the measure that I am putting out. When you understand this in your heart, you can feel compassion for the man or woman God has put in your life. You can feel empathy for this lifelong, fruitless effort. You can accept your loved one's freedom to do whatever he or she is doing. Most importantly, you can stop your half of the ping-pong struggle. You meet your lover wherever he or she is—Near or Far! You don't pressure her to meet you at the three foot mark. Furthermore, you don't slip into the trap of moving out to the forty foot mark, trying to outdistance her distance in the vain hope that this will pressure her to move closer.

When your partner punishes you with distance, what matters is how *you* respond. Can you love her where she is, not where you need her to be? When you are non-judgmental, you learn how to love your marriage partner as Jesus loves you—by giving him or her what is needed directly at your expense. You will willingly move to Far exactly when you really want her to be Near and close to you. Or, you will willingly move to Near, exactly when you really want to be Far, alone in your cave or on your island. This is *mercy* in action.

Jesus' death on the cross inspires us with his deep love for us. He selflessly took the penalty for our sins at his own expense. This deep lesson in humility lies hidden in the *Near* and *Far* dilemma in your marriage. When you make your needs as nothing the way Jesus did for us, then you will learn to love your spouse where she is, not where you "need" her to be. Your reward will be to deeply feel the love of Jesus and the grace of the Holy Spirit. As St. Francis of Assisi prayed,

"For it is in giving that we receive;

It is in pardoning that we are pardoned;

And it is in dying that we are born to eternal life."

Group Study: Compassion Lesson 3-5: Write out your "list." Be specific about every thing you want to change in your spouse. Then focus on accepting each one. Be intentional. Accept that not one of them will ever change—her weight, his criticisms of you, her emotional distance, his pre-occupations and her annoying habits. If you can't let them go, accept this too. You are not perfect. Your time will come when the Lord will help. Be ready to accept that time if and when it comes in your marriage or other personal relationships.

NOTES

3-6 Compassion Towards Self: Breaking an Addictive Habit

Compassion begins with compassion towards self. If you struggle to feel compassion towards others, you are probably quite hard on yourself. You may even justify your lack of generosity towards others by saying, "I don't ask anything that I wouldn't ask of myself!" This is self-righteous and suggests that "if I have to suffer and work hard, so should you!" This will reveal itself in the form of intolerance and a judgmental sense of superiority.

The key to breaking this form of judging others is to develop compassion towards yourself. This means to not judge your own weaknesses and faults. Nowhere is this struggle with oneself more evident than when you are dealing with an addiction. Addictions are habits that you can't break, no matter how hard you try. Indeed, the harder you try, the worse they get. Non-judgment reveals itself through surrendering. For anyone involved in alcoholism, the famous twelve step program is anchored in this one solution—full and complete surrender to your powerlessness to defeat your own bad habit.

Whether it is smoking, over-eating, over-working, alcohol, dope, sex or gambling, your addiction is your biggest opportunity to develop your own compassion and trust in God to do His work and show His great love for you. In the following story, God worked a miracle in my life and caused me to quit smoking when I stopped beating myself up to quit and fully surrendered to my weakness.

I began smoking when I was fourteen. I quit when I was twenty. Over the following twenty years, I started and quit smoking six more times, never smoking for more than a few months at a time. After hating myself for starting the fifth time, I began to embrace certain beliefs. The first belief I embraced was that I *want* to smoke. It was no longer a "need" or some outside force *making* me do it. I was doing it out of my own free will and my own choice. The second belief that I embraced was that I was choosing to smoke because in some way it was serving me *more* than not smoking. That was a hard one to get my head around, since the list of reasons to NOT smoke is so long. Nevertheless, I decided to believe that there must be a positive reason for doing it or else why would I do it? I fervently believe that I make my own choices. Therefore, smoking must serve me in some way.

One beautiful summer morning, I woke up with no cigarettes. I decided to walk down the street to the corner store to buy some more. As I walked along, I felt a great sense of joy and peace. The sun shone brightly, the birds sang beautifully, and the trees swayed gently in the soft breeze blowing in off Lake Ontario. After I bought my cigarettes, I walked along and lit one up. I immediately felt the "hit" as the smoke and nicotine entered my bloodstream. Within seconds, I noticed that the wonderful feeling that I had been enjoying was gone, replaced by a lightheaded dizziness and the beginnings of a small headache. At that moment, the reason smoking served me became clear to me. *Smoking numbed my emotions.*

I suddenly realized that each and every time I decided to start smoking again as a habit, one common thing was always present: *my emotions were at a high level of intensity.* Oddly enough, it didn't seem to matter if I felt really good, as I did that morning, or really terrible as I had on other occasions. If you talk to most smokers, they will tell you that smoking soothes them and calms their nerves. This is another way of saying that it numbs their emotional pain. I later came to understand that this numbing of emotions is the core benefit behind *all* addictions, whether it is sex, food, drugs or alcohol.

That afternoon, I walked over to a park and smoked my last cigarette. I felt very clear for the first time in my life about why I was quitting. It was no longer a battle between me and myself, as if this awful habit were a great struggle between good and evil. No, it was with a sense of peace that I was letting go of this addiction. I simply no longer wanted to numb my emotions. I wanted to feel my feelings to the fullest. I took my last drag, watched the smoke exhale out of my mouth for the last time, and threw the butt into the lake as a testimony to my "power" over this habit. Then I crushed the remaining cigarettes and tossed the whole works into a garbage can. It was that easy. My mind was at peace. I had no more doubts, and no more second thoughts about what I wanted.

Not smoking felt so easy after that. Just one month later, however, I stumbled. I had just settled my divorce and the intensity of how I was feeling crumbled my resolve—again! It was the third time I had started to smoke in the previous two years. To my great surprise, I did not feel judgmental of myself this time. I felt accepting of myself and the suffering and anguish that I was feeling following the settlement of my divorce. I was also surprised to notice that this time I did not feel a desire to hide it from others. I did not feel ashamed of my weakness and my failing. If others thought I was incredibly weak-willed, so be it. I accepted that I was smoking because it was serving me at some level that I could not yet understand. I felt confident that the purpose for my addiction would emerge sooner or later. I even decided to buy a pipe. The oral satisfaction of chewing on the end of that pipe was a comfort to me.

Four days before leaving for the upstate New York Christian festival called, *Kingdom Bound*, at two o'clock one morning, I experienced a moment of great clarity about my state of mind. I wrestled with a strong inner voice saying, *Go down to the car, get your cigarettes and have one.* I felt aware that I was really sleepy and could easily roll over and go to sleep. Instead, after several minutes, I went and got the smokes. I had three of them. I wrote in my journal, *"I am weak and I have failed. I don't feel shame. Just a sense of awareness of my battle. In the end, it is my decision. I feel I am inviting God to give me greater consequences—ones I won't want. Not for punishment, but rather more as tough love. Fatigue is my enemy. So is lack of physical activity. My physical well-being has fallen badly, as have my spiritual, emotional and mental well-being. And they are all so intertwined… I still seek control at some level. I have not fully submitted myself, my life to Jesus Christ. Too much remains intellectual. I hesitate to pray to God for strength. I have failed Him so often."*

On the first night of my arrival at Kingdom Bound, we began by going to see one speaker, a "healer." This woman spoke in tongues. After a period of time, people fell backwards into the waiting arms of friends. My brother-in-law himself did it. He wanted help to quit smoking. I looked at it without judgment, again to my surprise. For some reason, my skeptical, cynical voice was absent. *Who am I to say what God can and cannot do?* I thought to myself. Nevertheless, I saw no obvious miracles take place. That evening, a dozen of us sat around a campfire. I chatted with an attractive Christian woman who had also recently gone through a divorce. We carried on until two-thirty in the morning, talking about our divorces, our personal growth journeys, and our experiences with Christianity. I puffed on my pipe throughout the evening.

As I crawled into my tent late into the night under a dark and starlit sky, I felt tired and ready to instantly fall sleep. I decided to say a short prayer to God, to thank Him for the good day and the wonderful people camping with me. Suddenly and without warning, a voice clapped in my mind. *"I make a covenant with you to never smoke again."* I have never heard such a voice or felt such a deep conviction. This voice did not seem of my own doing. I had had no thoughts or intentions of quitting smoking. As fast as it happened, it was over. I fell fast asleep, aware that something quite powerful had just happened.

The next day, I woke up feeling very aware of this bolt of lightening event. I got up and told my sister Helen about what happened. I felt a bit embarrassed. A little voice inside me kept saying, *God talking in me? Yeah, right! Who's going to believe that?* Nevertheless, I decided to be real and tell her the story. She just nodded in response, having been a believer for fifteen years already. There was no doubt in her mind that this "bolt" could have come from God.

I then went about my normal routine. I was aware that I could have a cigarette, but I didn't really feel like having one just yet. I decided to go and spend the morning at two speaking sessions on topics that appealed to me. At noon, I came back to the campsite. Helen was there, smoking a cigarette. I sat down beside her.

As we chatted, I began to notice her cigarette. I was aware that I could ask her for a drag. I knew she would give it to me. I kept chatting, all the while noticing her cigarette. A voice in my head was saying, "Go ahead, have a drag. What's one drag?" I decided I would. I asked her for a puff, and she gave me a funny look. "Are you sure?" she asked. "I'm sure," I responded. I took the cigarette into my fingers. I could smell the smoke coming off the end of the butt. I brought the cigarette to my lips. This time, another thought spoke out very strongly and very clearly in my mind. *"I have made a covenant with God. I cannot and will not break it."* To my own amazement, I handed the cigarette back to Helen. "I can't do it," I said to her, "Not this time."

I have never smoked since. The next night, I surrendered my life to Jesus.

————————

Your ability to give compassion to others will be governed by your ability to give yourself support while you are suffering. The practical reality of this wisdom was captured in a study called The Marshmallow Study, done by Stanford University psychology researcher Michael Mischel in California in the 1960s. He took a group of young children and put them in a room with one marshmallow for each placed on a table. He then told them that if they could wait until he returned, they could have *two* marshmallows instead. About one third of the children immediately grabbed their marshmallows. The second third of them were able to wait several minutes before caving in. The final one-third of the children were able to endure the long and agonizing twenty minutes. All of these children were then tracked for many years thereafter. The ones who could delay their own need for instant gratification thrived at significantly higher levels in their careers and in life generally than the other children. The key to their success? Their ability to tell themselves that the wait was worth it, to turn away from temptation, and to endure. Your ability to support yourself while suffering will directly correlate with your ability to do the same for another, just as Jesus did for you.

Group Study: Compassion Lesson 3-6: What habit are you struggling with that you would like to change? Eating too much? Lack of exercise? Drinking too much? Obsessing about work? Fantasizing about sex? Whatever it is, what are you afraid would happen if you stopped trying to "quit," and just gave yourself support for doing it, accepting that you might never stop? Explore the possibility that you will never break this habit. How do you feel about that possibility? What beliefs are you holding that are self-judgmental?

NOTES

Lesson 4

YOU ARE WISE, NOT SMART

Annie barked at me expectantly. A fifty pound short-haired bull terrier, Annie was the most recent addition to our family. I petted her fondly amid the din of twenty other barking dogs and their rookie owners. I was still dismayed at discovering that in dog training school the one getting trained was me, not my dog!

"Can I have your attention please," the instructor hollered. Then she asked us to quiet our dogs in order for us to hear her lesson. She said, "Keep a handful of dog food pressed into your dog's mouth." Moments later, the room grew quiet.

Annie munched with delight. After about a minute, her warm slobber oozed onto my hand. Yuk! I decided to take my hand away to see if she would remain quiet. Within thirty seconds, Annie's alert eye spotted another dog moving and she barked. I immediately flashed my hand full of dogfood back to her mouth, embarrassed at disobeying my instructor's request. Instantly, Annie became quiet. Again, her slobbering began to bother me, so I pulled my hand away again, urging her to stay quiet. A minute later, she barked again. Immediately I put my hand back to her mouth to quiet her. This time I waited longer, listening to the instructor while enduring Annie's slimy dog saliva in the palm of my hand. I decided to try a third time. Within a minute, Annie once again barked. I quickly reached out to quiet her down when my instructor's eyes angrily locked onto mine. "YOU'RE TEACHING YOUR DOG TO BARK!" she hollered.

I was stunned. *Teaching my dog to bark? I am shutting her up!*

"Every time your dog barks, you are putting your hand to her mouth with dog food. For her, that's a reward for barking!" She sounded exasperated.

"Oh-h-h!" I groaned. *How dumb of me! I didn't even see it!*

I love this story because I see it happen so often in leadership situations with bosses, parents, spouses, teachers and anyone who wants to influence the behavior of another. We respond to people in ways that actually *cause* the very behavior we want to stop! We think we're *smart*, trying to get people to change in a certain way. Instead, we fail to be *wise*, blind to the real effects of our actions on others.

Our judgments are what blind us. I was triggered by my dog's barking, worried about being judged as a "disobedient student" by my instructor. I had *something to lose*—my reputation and self-respect. I was afraid of being judged by my instructor. This led me to be smart and seek an instant solution to Annie's barking. Smart means focusing on changing how people respond to you. Approving and disapproving is how we demonstrate our smartness. Wisdom means changing how you respond to people. Neither approving nor disapproving will open your eyes to being wise. The wise King Solomon offered us an example when he decided to cut the baby in half in order to settle the dispute between two women claiming to be one child's mother. He knew the real mother would not accept this and thereby discovered the truth without giving up, nor pressuring them. (1 Kings, Ch 3)

The purpose of this chapter is to learn how to influence the behavior of others to change, freely and willingly. Whether you are willing to admit or not, you are trying to influence other people's behavior every day. You are doing it when you honk your horn at a rude driver, ask your spouse to do an errand, discipline your child and ask your boss for a raise. Each of these is a leadership situation where you want others to follow you. When they do, you are happy. When they don't, you are often unhappy. What you do about your unhappiness will determine the quality of your relationships and the joy in your life.

I once did an on-line survey of husbands, asking them this one question: "What is the number one habit you want to change in your wife?" Just two of the twenty-two respondents said, *"Nothing. She is perfect as she is!"* Eleven husbands wanted her to change the way she communicated with him—*stop being bossy, nagging, crying too easily, being a know-it-all, not listening, and hiding her real feelings until she blows up.* Nine of the husbands wanted her to change her behavior—*smoking, drinking, spending, driving habits, not leaving things lying around, doing what she said she would do, and not misplacing things.*

Becoming skilled at influencing the behavior of the ones you love is crucial to the long term success of your marriage and raising your children. When you are weak in this area, you will lose hope in your relationship. **Losing hope is the main cause of divorce and broken relationships.** Without hope, despair sets in. Once despair sets in, one or both of you will feel that a turnaround is impossible.

You will have tried the hammer a "million" times. Then you will give up and become a doormat. Then you will walk away. This is a recipe for relationship disaster. Frustration, power struggles and emotional distance will dominate your life if you cannot master this important yet sensitive skill. In this chapter, you will see that being non-judgmental provides the platform to shift from neutral gear into spiritual gear. The "n-j way" will give you a firm "en-joy" foundation upon which to impact the lives of others for their benefit and your own peace of mind.

Non-judgment works because you build trust. You let go of your own agenda. You build trust by focusing on being helpful to them, while assertively respecting your own needs. On this basis, they will change for their own reasons and not because you pressured them. The acid-test for you will be if you are at peace if they don't change. They are free, and you are a helpful, Godly influence in their lives. This freedom is limited for children, of course, depending on their age and maturity. As parents, your boundaries overlap those of your growing children. How much your boundaries overlap and when to allow them to choose freely remains the challenge of being a parent! However, non-judgment will shift the way in which you influence the behavior of your children, as you will see by the stories in this chapter.

The practical application of leading your loved ones in this non-judgmental way is based on three leadership principles I have learned in the practical arena of home and business.

The first principle is the **Non-Judgment Principle:** You must first *eliminate* the judgments you have about someone's behavior that bothers you. If you fail in this first step, you will act while feeling judgmental and will most certainly do so with a Hammer. When you do, you will inflame the cycle of pain that Jesus warned us about in Mt 7:1, "And with the measure you use, it will be measured to you." (NIV) When you accept the freedom of others to act as they are acting, you will stop approving or disapproving of their behavior. This will engage the subsequent powerful leadership lesson from Jesus in Mt 7:5: "First take the plank out of your own eye, and then you will see clearly to remove the speck from your brother's eye." (NIV) With non-judgment, you will see what is important for you to do to be helpful to them.

The second principle is the **Act or Accept Principle:** You only ever have two leadership choices in any present moment situation—**Act or Accept**. If you neither act nor accept, you are choosing a third choice—the Doormat. You are sitting on the fence. Something they said or did bothers you but you suppress it, stew on it and let it eat away at you. Being a doormat is not being non-judgmental—it is being fake and a phony, and is a hammer in waiting.

The third leadership principle is **The W.I.N. Principle** (What's Important Now): **Support or Resist.** *Support* what is within their rights to do. *Resist* what is within your rights to resist. This principle is captured in the Steady Hands symbol revealed earlier.

When you follow these three principles, your actions will be wise. You will learn that by *not* trying to control, force or manipulate them, you will help them consider change of their own free will. They may even thank you afterwards, although if you are really good at this non-judgmental leadership skill, they won't even consider thanking you because from their perspective, they did it themselves! If this is your experience, you will have achieved your highest goal as a leader—that your loved ones will make real and meaningful changes because it was *their* idea, not yours.

I had the joy of this experience with my seven year old son and his struggles playing hockey one long, cold winter.

4-1 Improved Performance: An Under-Achieving Child

As parents, we want our children to excel. Personally, I want my children to give their best effort, even if that effort doesn't yield all-star results. It is the effort that matters. The school marks and athletic achievements will naturally follow to the peak of their God-given talents, regardless of how they compare to any other kid.

My seven year old son Jared was in his second year of playing minor house league hockey. His first year was a good one by all measures. He scored several goals and played with confidence and skill. His coaches ranked him above average and he graduated into the highest level of house league in his second year. As the second year began, however, something changed for Jared. While he made a good effort at practices, he faded when the real game began. He put out a minimal effort, rarely even touching the puck unless it happened to hit his stick by chance. He appeared to have little interest in the game, and backed away when the action got too close to him. The only time he showed energy was when the buzzer sounded, at which point he would skate full-blast to the bench in order to be the first to sit down!

I was quite bothered by his performance. I knew I felt judgmental by the simple fact that I had to restrain myself from wanting to be the overbearing Dad who gets on his son's case, pressuring him to try harder! Instead, I sat on it for several weeks. I was in Doormat mode and I knew it, as I struggled to figure out what to do. Finally, after a particularly weak game, I decided to Act because I knew I was not Accepting his lackluster effort. I suggested to him that I didn't think he was trying very hard. He immediately felt hurt, saying to me in near tears, "I am *so* trying hard! I'm doing the best that I can Dad!" I backed off instantly. I had slipped into traditional Hammer leadership and his defensive reaction confirmed that to me.

Instead, I went back to my first leadership principle: How could I accept his non-effort, that is, be non-judgmental about it? I started noticing my judgmental thoughts. I noticed that I worried about what the other parents might be thinking of him as they cheered and groaned in the stands. I noticed my impulsive desire to shout instructions at him from the stands. I notice that I worried about being seen as one of *those* loud-mouthed hockey parents. I had to accept that my desire to control his play on the ice was very strong. I even admitted to myself that part of me wanted to look good in the eyes of others through my son's conquests on the ice. I reminded myself that it was all for fun, that Jared was doing the best he could and most importantly, that his performance was not a reflection of me. I had *nothing to lose* if he played poorly!

Finally, I felt ready to Act. I wanted to do so in accordance with the WIN Principle. Was there anything for me to *resist*? Nothing! He was free to play the game any way that he wanted. My only real choice was to *support* him. I had to find a way to influence his performance that was genuinely supportive and non-pressuring.

After another ho-hum game, I asked him how well he thought played.

He answered, "Great, Dad."

I thought to myself, *That is amazing, He is blind to himself!* A sudden inspiration struck me. "Your bicycle has seven gears right?"

"Yeah," he answered.

"What gear would you say you were skating in?"

He thought about it for a moment. "About sixth gear," he said confidently.

I looked over at him with surprise, biting my tongue as we drove home from the arena. "Would you like to know what gear I think you were in?"

"Okay," he said.

I started with a positive behavior that I had noticed. "I think you were in about sixth gear when you skated off the ice. That was really good. The rest of the time, I would say you were in second gear." I said it rather matter-of-factly. I watched for his reaction. He looked straight ahead, taking it in. "Really?" he pondered.

"Yeah, I think so. Do you notice the difference that I'm talking about?"

"Yeah, I suppose…" He sounded skeptical. I left it at that.

The next game, I asked him if he was willing to see if he could get into sixth gear. He said he would. I said I would count the number of times he did it. After the game, I asked him what gear he thought he reached. He said, "Fourth mostly. I did hit sixth gear on that one play at center ice!" I agreed with him, and felt pleasantly surprised at how the simple technique of giving him an objective measure had helped him see himself quite a bit more accurately.

Two games later, his skating remained much more energetic but he still avoided the puck. He appeared to not want to get bumped by the other players, something he admitted to me one time. Finally, one of his little teammates came up to him after the game and said, "Hey Jared, what are you doing out there? Are you asleep on the ice?" I was standing right there. Jared said, "Yeah, maybe," as he fiddled with the pop machine.

When I asked him later if that comment bothered him, he said, "Nah-h. I didn't mind."

"Well that's good," I replied. I had no intention of rescuing him but I did want to know if he felt hurt. Personally, I was glad his teammate had spoken up. I call that a "natural consequence," one of a leader's most effective tools to help someone to change freely and willingly. Natural consequences work wonderfully well if you are able to be empathetic, not sympathetic. With empathy, you affirm your support for them without attempting to fix, change, alter or rescue them from the pickle they've created for themselves.

With just three weeks left in the season, I had another inspiration. This happened right after I truly accepted that Jared might not *ever* pick up his pace. I even accepted that he could quit hockey altogether. For the first time, the Lord revealed to me the way to remove the speck from my son's eye. I began to see the actual behavior that I wanted to help him change. I needed to find a way to encourage him to actually *hold on* to the puck. I estimated that Jared held the puck for about three seconds per game. With some thought about what leadership tool I might use to accomplish this end, I decided to offer him an incentive. I offered him one Yu-gi-oh card (a kid's card game he loved)—for every second that he had control of the puck.

He reacted to this idea with great delight! The next game, he held on to the puck for fourteen seconds in total, *a nearly five times improvement.* He came off the ice glowing, eagerly telling me that he had held on to it for twenty seconds! I empathized with his mistaken math and then bought him fourteen cards right after the game. He said to the store clerk, "Yeah. Not only did I get to buy cards, but I even had more fun playing hockey!"

This was exactly the effect I was hoping for. He discovered he could do more than he thought which is a helpful, confidence-building experience. The secret to this kind of supportive leadership is to not institutionalize it. Otherwise, people begin to perform only for the incentive and stop when it gets removed. I wanted him to learn a new skill, not find a way to earn cards! For that reason, I removed the card offer after that one game. However, I kept feeding back to him his "puck control time." This became a new focal point for him after every game. His puck control time steadily rose game by game to twenty seconds, a very satisfying improvement.

Then we entered a three game tournament on an out-of-town weekend venture with the team. *He seems stalled again*, I thought. I wanted to motivate him to move one notch higher by getting a shot on net, something he had not done all year long. In the third and final game, I decided to offer him a full pack of nine cards for every shot on net he got. He gladly accepted the challenge. To my disappointment however, he did very little throughout the game. Even his puck control went down. With a little over a minute left in the game, he was on the ice with this big game tied at 2-2. The parents in the stands gave the players a rousing cheer and Jared playfully danced to their chant just before the referee dropped the puck.

Suddenly, he came to life. He skated out front, got the puck and took a hard shot on net. It was his very first shot on net of the year! I was thrilled, suppressing my mild disappointment at what a great opportunity it would have been for him if he had scored. Fifteen seconds later, he was knocked down. As he rose up on one knee, the puck came to him again. Without hesitating, he fired a hard shot. The puck streaked past the outstretched goalie and hit the back of the net. The red light went on and the crowd went wild! His team won the game 3-2 and he had scored the game-winning goal, his first goal of the year. When the three stars of the game were announced, Jared proudly stepped forward to receive the bronze medal as the third star of the game. His confidence soared and he played like a new kid in the final game of the season.

Any leader can shape another person's behavior if they are willing to first set aside their judgments about that person's behavior. My executive coaching clients experience the power of non-judgment in seeing creative new ways to influence the people they work with. One of my clients whom I'll call Richard was fed up with his partner whom I'll call Gary. Gary was under-performing and wreaking havoc in the office. He had the upsetting habit of storming into meetings uninvited and dumping all over every one else's ideas. For two years Richard tried to get his emotionally volatile partner to stop this behavior. Every couple of months, he had calm, logical talks with Gary. Each time, Gary would obligingly agree to stop his disruptive intrusions. Within two weeks, he would do it again. Richard spent the better part of four months coaching with me on a weekly basis in order to break this endless, frustrating cycle. The first goal of my coaching was to help Richard see the world through his partner's eyes—Gary's frustration at his lack of success, his ego need to be the "star" and his basic character as an emotional and erratic person.

Literally the week after Richard felt a good measure of peace and compassion for Gary, he had an "inspiration." He called me to tell me he had decided to change both his own job structure and that of his partner. He told me with great conviction that he intended to resign if Gary didn't accept his proposal. This was an excellent example of a Resist tactic. To Richard's delight, his proposal was warmly greeted Gary, and he never had to use his back up plan. Nevertheless, knowing he had one that he felt good about was central to his ability to calmly and confidently lay out his plan without being manipulative. The underlying key to Richard's success was that he was being real. He had hit the end of his rope. He explored and accepted the risks of finding new work and dealing with the financial fallout. His willingness to exit the business himself meant that this was not a coercive threat. He was at peace with it, which is the key measure of non-judgmental leadership. Four months after that, Gary left the firm of his own free will. This was exactly the outcome Richard wanted. As they were long-time friends outside the business, Richard was especially happy with this delightful win-win result.

Group Study: Wisdom Lesson 4-1: Break down your goals into tiny, one inch parts. Remember that your inch is often their yard. Break down the task into tiny parts, in order to see just how small an inch really can be. Begin with tying your shoelace. Become aware that every task is a process, from putting on pants to building an entire house. Notice your own difficulties when you are learning a new skill. This will keep you humble, positive and supportive of your loved ones as they struggle for days, weeks, months and even years to do what may come so easily for you.

NOTES

4-2 Repairing a Damaged Relationship: Father and Son

Smart people already know the answer. Wise people let the Lord lead them to the answer. The key to this most practical aspect of being an influential leader begins with one basic principle: **You become willing to change some of your deeply held beliefs.**

Beliefs are the basis upon which we make judgments. They are our rule book about how things "should" be. We compare the present moment to our beliefs and instantly get triggered by what's happening. My first wife and I were house-aholics at one time. We drove around on weekends to visit open houses and scout out nice neighborhoods. I would spot a house that I liked and ask her, "*Don't* you love the porch on that house?" This is called a loaded question. How could she disagree? My opinion (judgment) about that house was carved into the words I was using as well as my tone of voice. If she disagreed, I would often begin arguing with her, trying to convince her that she was failing to see the obvious beauty of my choice and why the heck couldn't she just admit that and agree with me! My question reflected my underlying belief that *I have to have the right answer.* I felt threatened if she didn't confirm to me that I was right, even though logically I knew that there was no "right" or "wrong" answer about the kind of house that a person prefers.

Beliefs are not inherently logical. They just automatically trigger an emotional response that appears in the form of a judgment. Every feeling you have that is annoying, frustrating, maddening, worrying and even gleeful, can be linked to a belief and a judgment. Until you become aware of your underlying beliefs and change them, you will remain trapped in the Hammer or Doormat dilemma, wanting to lash out at others who trigger your beliefs, or resentfully suppress what you really think and feel.

This next story is the gut-wrenching tale of an adult son reconciling with his father after fifteen years of being distant and superficial. During that long time, he was blinded by his beliefs about what fathers *should* do for their sons and his resulting judgments of him. Then the Lord sent him an instructor to open his eyes, fill him with courage, and give him one of the greatest gifts of a person's life—a warm, open, loving relationship with his or her father.

I was in the seventh week of the eight week personal growth program I mentioned earlier in this book. We were continuing our on-going work of breaking down our emotional walls of judgments. Once again, we were asked to look into the eyes of a classmate. I found myself looking at "Present," an attractive, dark-haired single woman in her mid-thirties. She reminded me of myself—sort of analytical and a bit of a cold fish. As I gazed into her eyes that day, I felt overwhelmed with the feeling that she was just a little girl, terribly hurt and all alone. My eyes grew watery with tears and my throat became thick as my emotions welled up. My instructor noticed and asked why. I told him about how Present was triggering me. He asked, "Do you really think you can feel the hurts of another person?" By now, I had accepted a new belief that my feelings were about me, and not others.

"No, I guess not," I said quietly.

"So what is this about?" he asked gently.

I paused. "I guess it's about my dad," I reluctantly offered. "I feel like he abandoned me and what did I do to deserve that?" I fought back the tears in my eyes as I had stoically done since I was thirteen years old.

"Why are you holding on to this?" he asked.

"I guess it's been a part of me for so long. I've kept hoping that by being distant with him, he would reach out to me."

"Has it worked?" the instructor asked in his usual gentle yet frank manner.

"Absolutely not." I was blunt. I had nothing to hide anymore.

"So why do you keep doing it?

I hesitated. Why? My stomach suddenly had that sinking feeling. "I guess by blaming him, I don't have to be responsible for improving our relationship. You know, it's all his fault." I was stunned by this moment of self-revelation.

He went on. "What are you afraid might happen if you were to let this go?

I hesitated, feeling overwhelmed by what I was suddenly seeing. "I might admit that I love him and need him."

"How do you feel about that prospect?"

"I'm afraid he would reject me." My chest ached as I held back a tidal wave of emotion.

"What would you like to say to your father if he were here?"

I considered his question for a few moments. "I'd say, 'I want a meaningful relationship with you where we talk about how we feel and not just the weather.'"

Suddenly a sparkle appeared in my instructor's eye. "Are you willing to do an experiment with me?"

"Sure," I said quietly, knowing he would make me face this one even further. I was not at all sure that I was ready to go there but my trust level was high by that time.

"Repeat what you just said as if your father were sitting right here in the middle of this room."

I dutifully cooperated. "Dad, I want a meaningful relationship with you where we talk about how we feel and not just the weather."

Instantly the class responded in unison. "Not interested!" I was stunned by the force of their unexpected words, and oblivious as to how my instructor had coached them on.

"Say it again," he urged me.

I took a deep breath. "Dad, I want a meaningful relationship with you where we talk about how we feel and not just the weather."

"NOT INTERESTED!" The class boomed back at me.

"Say it again," Bears said.

I was getting annoyed. "Dad, I want a meaningful relationship with you where we talk about how we feel and not just the weather."

This time the class response was deafening. "**NOT INTERESTED!!!**"

Anger surged throughout my entire being. I shook as I did everything in my power to maintain my calm. My instructor looked at me calmly. "What's coming up for you?"

"What's coming up for me is a great big F— You!" I blurted out angrily.

"Why is that?" he asked patiently.

"If you reject me, I'll reject you," I snarled, filled with conviction to the marrow of my bones.

"Does that get you what you want?" he asked in his quizzical way.

My heart sunk like a stone. The force of his question nearly knocked me over. I suddenly saw truth and it hurt. "No, it doesn't…" My voice trailed off. The impact of that moment penetrated to my soul.

My instructor asked me if I was willing to do some homework. I agreed. I mean, why not? The guy had taken me this far down this road. I was still reeling from the revelation that I had been holding a judgmental belief about my father that if I was just distant enough, he would chase after me. For the last fifteen years I believed that! What a fool I had been!

For my homework, my instructor suggested that I call my father and tell him exactly what I had said to the class. I said, "I can do better than that. I'm going home this very weekend. I'll do it live!" He smiled at my enthusiasm and then gave me a word to the wise, "Let him respond in whatever way he wants and just accept it. If he isn't interested, love him anyway. In fact, double it!" I have *nothing to lose*, I thought. I agreed to do it and report back to class the next week.

I arrived at home on Friday night with the perfect opportunity to speak up. My dad and I were sitting in the living room, chatting idly. I was really scared. My heart was pounding. *I cannot do it!* So I thought, *Fine, I'll do it tomorrow.* The next morning, I had another perfect opportunity to do it. The mere thought of speaking up sent wave after wave of fear coursing through my body. I simply could not get up the nerve to speak up. *All right,* I thought, *I'll wait until Sunday morning.* Sunday morning arrived. I knew this was my last chance before I had to head back to class and to my instructor's inquiring voice. I had another perfect opportunity as the two of us sat in the family room, twenty minutes before he and my mother were to go to church. I chickened out again! I had never felt such terror in all of my life as I felt at the prospect of reaching out to my father. All I could imagine was me saying *I need you* and him sneering in my face, saying, "*There you are, still the weak little boy you always were!*"

As my parents prepared to go to church, I decided to stay behind. I wrestled with what to do. I decided to begin my daily meditation. Three minutes into it, the inspiration came to write him a letter instead. In this shortened version, I began:

Dear Dad,

I love you. I have been afraid my whole life to tell you that. I always focused on your negatives rather than the many good things you did for me and taught me. I learned so much from you, including a good work ethic and many trade skills that I value very much. I have always admired you, your hard work, your many accomplishments and your sense of humor. I also want you to know how much it meant to me when you helped me buy my first car and my first house.

These last many years, I have been distant from you in the silly hope that you would reach out to me. I avoided the very thing I wanted, which is to have a good relationship with you. Today, I'm thirty nine and you're sixty-seven. We are not parent/child anymore. I want to be friends. If either one of us were to die in the next six months, is there anything you would want to have said to me? If so, please feel free to speak up now. There is nothing you can say or do that will change the fact that I love you and I want to be there for you. I am always impressed by how caring and giving you are towards others, especially towards me at this time [my marriage breakdown]. You are a gift to me and to all of us around you.

With love,
John

When he walked in the door from church, I did not dare to hesitate. As soon as he came in the room, I handed him the letter. He sat down and began to read it. He looked up half way through it and smiled. "This is nice." When he finished reading, he looked up at me and said, "This is really nice. Thank you." He paused for a moment. "There is one thing I do want to talk about."

My heart sunk like a stone. *Oh no, what did I do?* For a moment, I was seven years old all over again. "What's that?" I asked, reminding myself that his feelings were about him and not me.

"When I was in the hospital two months ago for my surgery, it really hurt me that your sisters and all the grandkids came to see me and you didn't even call me." Then he started to cry deep, racking sobs. "I know you were in Florida and you have all kinds of problems but it hurt anyway."

I went semi-numb. This was the last thing I expected. My mind flashed back. He had been in hospital overnight for corrective prostate surgery. I had called him the next day when he returned home. A flash of guilt crossed my heart. Then I let it go. Justifying my actions was definitely not what was important now. Indeed, I was in awe. Here was the best man I ever knew, showing his true feelings in a way that I knew I was not capable of myself. He grew another foot taller in my eyes in that moment. I walked over and quietly put my hand on his knee. Then I took a deep breath. "I'm sorry, Dad. I just wasn't thinking."

He grew calm. "I guess it was just something I had to get off my chest."

I spoke quietly, "I made a mistake and I'd do it differently now if I could."

My mother looked over at me. "We've all made a lot of mistakes." And then we gave each other a big three-way hug.

My relationship with my father has blossomed since then. We have real conversations about real things in our lives now. I no longer feel nervous about how he might react to anything I might say or do. We no longer have one-way conversations where he does all the talking and I resentfully listen like a Doormat. I stopped being "smart" and started being wise. I decided what I wanted and I pursued it, facing my deep fear that he would reject and humiliate me. This was my past, rearing its ugly head. It was a past that proved to be irrelevant and not predictive in this new present moment. What a joyous place to be! But to get there, I had to overcome my deeply engrained belief that rejecting him would somehow get him to love me. I also had to face another belief—that I would crumble if he rejected me when I was vulnerable with him.

You cannot wisely influence your relationships if you remain stuck on beliefs about what "he should've" or "she should've" done. You must risk the possibility that someone will judge your real feelings and hopes. When that person is your parent, you are reaching out to the person who has taught you most of your judgmental beliefs, whether they know it or not. These beliefs are deeply embedded in your unconscious mind, triggering your deepest fears. Until you face them, they will block you from loving your parents exactly as they are, in spite of whatever mistakes they made while raising you. When you accept your mother's faults or your father's faults, you honor them, just as the Bible commands. Then, as Jesus promised, you will receive back in the measure that you give. For me, the reward of a warm relationship with my father has made every hour, every dollar and every scary moment that I have spent on this journey worthwhile.

Group Study: Wisdom Lesson 4-2: Identify beliefs that are blocking a close relationship. Write down the person you would like to reach. Then ask yourself what you want. Does the relationship matter enough to reach out? If they died tomorrow, are you confident you would be at peace? If so, accept that. If not, write down what upsets you about them. Be aware that judgments get foggy—we forget why we're judgmental. We only know we are! Focus on forgiving them for how they hurt you. Can you begin to see your own role in the breakdown? Can you own just that, without feeling a need to "get them" to admit their own role? If not, you are not ready. Stay with this until you feel completely at peace. Then the Lord will reveal to you what action you should take, if any.

NOTES

_____

_____

_____

_____

_____

4-3 How to Influence People to Change, Freely & Willingly

Jesus was a leader whom people followed, freely and willingly. "Come, follow me," Jesus said, "and I will make you fishers of men." At once, they left their nets and followed him." (MT 4:19-20 NIV) Is this how leadership works for you? You say, "Jump" and they say, "How high?" Maybe if you're the big boss at work! But at home, we don't have that kind of power and authority. For many of us, the struggle to get loved ones to do what we want is a frustrating experience that leads to heartache, resentment, conflict, and broken relationships.

When you want someone to change their behavior, you are being a leader. Whether you succeed or not is measured by whether the person follows you. **The important question is: Are you succeeding?** Does your child _stop_ whining when he doesn't get what he wants? Does your father _start_ having real conversations with you? Do your loved ones _keep going_ when they're facing adversity? Does your wife _keep_ talking to you when she gets upset?

Leadership is measurable, and there are the _only_ three measures. I call these the Leadership Traffic Light:

1. **Red Light:** People STOP repeating an old habit that is no longer useful.

2. **Yellow Light:** People START a new behavior that is useful.

3. **Green Light:** People KEEP DOING what they know is right, even when they would rather give up.

If you feel frustrated with someone, you can be sure that it is because you are *failing* to achieve your leadership goals. You are not successfully getting the other person to Stop, Start, or Keep Doing something that matters to your success and happiness. Is your wife critical of you? Does she keep her distance from you? Does your husband do the opposite of what you want? Do your children have habits you would like to change? Do the people you work with resist new ideas? Are you frustrated with how your parents treat you? Does your spouse keep threatening to leave you? Each of these is a leadership challenge. Your ability to motivate real changes in others will grow when you embrace one basic leadership principle:

By the yard, it's hard. By the inch, it's a cinch!
We fail as leaders because we want change to happen *by the yard*. We want sweeping changes and we want it now. We want major "transformational" changes in others—more respect, more thoughtfulness, more motivation, less moodiness, more discipline, less criticism, and so on. We want people to do things the way we do things, and to do it rapidly, easily and enthusiastically.

When our loved one fails to respond to our needs quickly enough, out come the Hammer and the Doormat. These tools often work, but at the cost of breaking down trust and building up resentment. Paul counseled leaders with these wise words: "Masters, act in the same way toward them [slaves], and stop bullying, knowing that both they and you have a Master in heaven and that with Him there is no partiality." (EPH 6:9 NAB)

When I coach people, I ask them how long they have been trying to get someone to change. They often react with surprise at the question. Upon reflection, they realize that they have been trying for two years, five years, even fifteen years to get a loved one or colleague to change, without *any* meaningful success!

I asked one client what was bothering him about his wife. He said, "She's such a slob!" I asked him if he could do "slob" for me.

He looked at me somewhat strangely. "What do you mean?" he asked.

"I mean can you do 'slob' behavior?"

"Sure," he said, picking up his papers and throwing them all over the floor.

"Is that 'slob' or is that leaving papers all over the floor?"

His eyes lit up. "Papers all over the floor, of course."

"Okay," I said, "so what do you really want from her in behavioral terms?"

"I guess I want her to not leave dirty, wet towels lying all over the bathroom floor."

"Ah-h, now you have a real leadership goal. How long have you wanted her to do this?"

He grimaced. "Oh, about ten years!"

"And what have you done to get her to stop that habit?"

"I've asked her about a million times!" he said, the resentment rising in his voice.

"And is it working?" I asked.

He face grew ashen. "No. It's not working."

After a few moments, I asked him, "Do you know what the definition of insanity is?"

"No, what is it?" he asked, grinning sheepishly.

"It's when you keep doing the same thing over and over, expecting to get a different result!" He laughed.

For most couples, marriage includes a power struggle. Each partner wants to get his or her needs met, based on each person's own deeply held, long engrained beliefs about how things "should" be. Whether it is how towels are left behind, how money gets spent, or how often they have sex, these are boundary battles that say, *If you really loved me, you would meet my needs.* Judgments are the evidence that one partner wants to shift the other person's boundaries. We try to get the other person to change about "a million times." Then we give up in frustration. The hammer and doormat cycle repeats itself over and over. These judgments, big and small, accumulate like snowflakes that become snowballs that become an avalanche. The avalanche is the tragedy of separation and divorce. The equally disturbing alternative is conflict avoidance. This creates a roommate relationship that is distant and devoid of real love.

Your marriage involves two people who are "reinforcing" each other's behavior in a positive way or a negative way. Criticizing your mate's habits inspires him or her to... DIG IN! Saying nothing inspires them to... DO NOTHING! The key to getting what you want in any relationship is to notice your role in the struggle and focus on changing your own behavior. When you are judgmental, you are saying to the other person, "You change and I'll stay the same." Non-judgmental leadership says, "You're free to stay the same and I will change." Paul encourages us in Philippians 2:3, "Do nothing out of selfish ambition or vain conceit, but in humility consider others better than yourselves. Each of you should look not only to your own interests but also to the interests of others." (NIV)

So how does Non-judgmental Leadership work?

First, remove the plank from your eye. Become non-judgmental about each issue that bothers you. Notice the "labels" you use to describe what upsets you about your loved one. Set these aside and look at the actual behavior you wish were different. What words do they say or not say? What actions do they do or not do? Make it your goal to understand how it serves the other person to be that way. This is the foundation for empathy and compassion. Accept that he or she is free to be that way, and that his or her behavior is not meant to hurt you. In acting out the behavior, the person is merely being who he or she is. The behavior is not about you. You must surrender your needs by having *nothing to lose* if you don't get what you want.

Second, focus on the inch. What is the new behavior you want to encourage? Decide clearly if changing it matters enough to you to invest time and energy with this person. Pray for wisdom and insight that what you want is good for the person, and not merely serving your own selfish needs. Feeling guilty that you are being selfish (which is a judgment in itself) will block your ability to execute these techniques.

Third, get clear about boundaries. Is this their space or your space? What is within the realm of your space to Resist, and theirs to Support? If it is theirs, you are in danger of being a watermelon. Give thanks for the opportunity to be humble and accept that any change the other person makes will be a gift from the Lord, and is not your right to receive. This will give you a clear framework for the next step.

Fourth, decide on a plan. Be intentional. Your goal is to *lift* your loved one to a higher level, not to manipulate him or her. Then break down the behavior into small parts. If you want the person to stop being late, decide what the first step is. Perhaps it is that *the other person* set the arrival time, not you. Perhaps the second step is to help him or her become self-aware of the fact that he/she keeps missing their own timing. Then you might coach the person to recognize new ways for arriving on time. Perhaps you need to resist and start without the person when he or she arrives late. Wisdom gets creative once you see your purpose as lovingly helping the person rather than resentfully pushing him or her into doing things your way.

Here are four tools to add to your leadership tool box that will encourage real behavior change from the person, freely & willingly.

1. **Give empathy**—Their change involves pain. If you can provide compassion instead of well-meaning solutions, you will give people the emotional support that they are unable to give to themselves (or they wouldn't be in pain about the change in the first place).
2. **Catch them doing it right.** Your support of the person's own free-will behavior will encourage him or her. Simple as this sounds, many leaders struggle with this. You must get past your judgmental belief that the other person is "only doing what they should have been doing in the first place!" Don't criticize the shortfalls and ignore the successes. Do the opposite.
3. **Don't take any credit.** If your loved one changes, resist the temptation to point out your role in his or her success. The change belongs to the person and to God's Spirit working in him or her. All you are is His instrument. This is your duty and your privilege: you are loving people, not rescuing them.
4. **Accept their freedom to not change.** This is the foundation. You must have nothing to lose. If you have something to lose, you will inexorably want to pressure people to change out of fear that you won't get what you want, be it emotional sustenance, financial security, tasks done on time, or cherished dreams realized.

Leading people is a creative art. Each situation requires separate thought and effort. This is why leaders fail. They want one sweeping solution that changes the other person permanently. This is delusional, prideful thinking. If the issue bothers you enough, it is worth investing time and experimenting with it. Complaining is your evidence that you are neither acting, nor accepting. You are being a doormat!

The following is a list of additional leadership tools that will get your creative juices flowing towards achieving your leadership goals with a loved one or anyone. Like any skill, each tool requires practice and experience. You must be willing to make mistakes. You must also become skilled at rapidly switching from tool to tool as needed, like a carpenter who knows just which tool to use moment by moment. Finally, remember that these leadership tools will be very difficult to do if you are merely suppressing your real judgments. At best, they will result in manipulation that will come back to bite you later when people see through your hypocrisy:

To STOP old habits: A person's irritating habit works for them, even if it is self-defeating or destructive. For example, he or she complains a lot, but doesn't do anything about it.

1. **Ignore it.** Reaction of any kind is often a reward that reinforces the old habit (resist)
2. **Empathize.** You hear and understand, but you don't fix. (support & resist)
3. **Substitute** a new habit for the old one. ie. "I'm not available to hear complaints in that way, but I will in *this* way." (resist)
4. **Set up a cue.** Whether it is a raised eyebrow or a simple "uh-uh," establish a way to communicate "no thanks." (resist)
5. **Assert what you want.** Be gentle, firm and consistent. Your loved one is not a mind-reader. Remember, old habits die hard. (resist)
6. **Use natural consequences.** Allow people to experience the reality that the old way doesn't get them what they want. (resist)
7. **Turn the habit into a positive.** You could reframe his complaints by saying, "You are so *creative!*" rather than judging him as *critical and unsupportive.* (support)
8. **Make it a behavior you can laugh at.** i.e. "She likes to nag and I like to let her." This is proof that you really are non-judgmental and she is free to be that way. She will hear your feedback without feeling threatened and consider changing of her own free will. (support)

9. **Take the hit.** If you are the one they are complaining about, *agree* with the person. Do it fully and completely, without watering it down by saying, "I didn't mean to." Once you've agreed, there is nothing left to complain about. This doesn't mean you will agree to change. You are helping them accept that complaining doesn't work, so *give it up*!

To START new behaviors: You must proceed with the understanding that they don't know how to do it and need your help to grow into it. You must see yourself as their coach, helping them to excel! For example, you want them to listen more and not take over the conversation.

1. **Model the behavior yourself.** Watch out for *All I See is Me*. *Be sure* that you yourself are doing what you want from them. (support)
2. **Notice and praise the behavior when it happens.** (support)
3. **Ask them.** "Are you willing to listen for a full minute?" Be at peace if you have to ask each time. Let go of the fact that it's the "millionth time" you've asked. (resist)
4. **Coach them.** Use open-ended questions to help them see new ways to do what you want, such as writing down their idea that they can't wait to tell you. (support)
5. **Never say, "You always…"** or "You never…" which are judgmental, global statements that trigger a defensive reaction. (support)
6. **Ask permission to help.** Don't give unasked for advice or tell them answers they don't want. Be aware that all new habits involve going through a learning curve. (support)
7. **Let them stumble.** Mistakes are normal! Empathize when it happens, or ignore it. Focus on catching them doing it right instead! (resist)
8. **Invite blind trust.** Ask their permission for you to walk through exactly what you want from them. Get over the judgmental belief that "They should know what I want without my having to tell them!" (support)
9. **Connect what you want to a unifying vision or purpose.** i.e. "Getting good at this will build our marriage in a huge way." (support)
10. **Use an incentive.** Offer a temporary reward to begin the new behavior. You can be very creative here if you keep things light and fun. Non-judgment will help you get over feeling uncomfortable about trying new ideas, just

because they're new. Just don't institutionalize your idea as a new "rule"! (support)

To KEEP DOING tried & true behaviors: They know how to do it but want to quit. For example, you want your children to do their homework.

1. **Give specific feedback.** Notice how they overcame a particular struggle, found a creative solution or made something happen. Be specific and timely (support).
2. **Empathize.** They have their reasons why they would rather quit. (resist & support)
3. **Fall on your sword.** In their mind, you may be partially to blame for their struggle. Take the hit if they blame you i.e "There may be an element of truth in what you're saying." (support)
4. **Notice what gets them interested and do that more often.** One man told me his wife gets turned on when he's wearing a suit. Wear a suit more often! Be playful! (support)
5. **Don't nag.** Ask if there is any way you can be helpful, short of actually doing it for them. (support)
6. **Join in with them.** Participate in the task while always making sure they are the driver and you are merely the helpful passenger. Never take over the task. (support)
7. **Give random rewards.** Celebrate with flowers, a card, dinner, or a gift to people for being who they are, not for any specific behavior. This is like making deposits in your relationship bank account. (support)
8. **Focus on the process.** Let go of the outcome. What does the person need at this very moment? Ignore whining. Focus them on the immediate task of picking up the pencil or opening the book. (resist)
9. **Keep your eye on the issue.** Avoid red herrings that derail the conversation. Let go of your attachment to whether the end result happens on time or at all. Just focus on getting the immediate inch in front of you done. (resist)

People often fear that if they are non-judgmental, they will become like a monk on a mountain top who merely watches the world pass by without making an impact on others. In truth, the opposite is what happens. When you stop judging a person or situation, you will feel courage to take bold, assertive action because you are doing it *with love in your heart*. More often than not, people will do what you want when you approach them in this way. You will see that the actions you take will often be far different from what you used to do when you were blinded by your judgmental disapproval, criticism and unhappiness.

If you become non-judgmental and then fail to *act*, you are merely a non-judgmental bump on a log. This is far from what Jesus did! Non-judgment gives you the courage to shift gears in the opposite direction by taking greater risks. Then you will become a coach and teacher who influences your loved ones to follow your lead freely and willingly...or not at all!

Group Study: Wisdom Lesson 4-3: Coach a new behavior with a loved one. Start small, such as navigating them through homework or learning to put away dirty dishes. Then increase the challenge. If you have a skill for a hobby, become their teacher. Teach them to play a musical instrument that you know how to play yourself. Notice what discourages them and what encourages them. Consider in your youth, who was your favorite teacher or coach? What qualities did that person possess? Did one of your parents or grandparents invest time to teach you skills you value even today? How do you feel about those who did...and those who did not?

NOTES

4-4 Get Them to Follow the Rules: A Work Situation

Judgments are everywhere, and that includes the work environment. This next story is about a Christian group home for female teens. Not surprisingly, the agency needs to maintain and enforce certain "rules of the house" in order to properly staff the home and create a safe, supportive living environment for these young women during a challenging time in their lives. My heart was touched by their compassion and commitment to their cause. One day, I spoke with one of the administrators.

"How is it going?" I asked curiously over the phone.

"Okay," answered my friend Joan. "I *am* feeling a little frustrated, though, I must admit.

"What are you frustrated about?" I asked.

"Oh, one of the residents has been breaking the rules. She doesn't tell us if she's going out on the weekend, and if she does, she comes in late or pulls a no show. I've had to issue her a letter that says, *'If I fail to live up to my agreement, I MAY be asked to leave the home.'* As nothing had changed, I finally had to write, *'WILL be asked to leave the home."*

"Wow, that's tough," I said sympathetically. My curiosity was instantly aroused at what appeared to be her use of traditional "Hammer-type" leadership.

"Yeah, it is," Joan responded. "I hated to do it, but what else could I do?"

"Do you mind if I ask you what she's been doing?" I asked. "I may be able to be helpful to you here."

"No, I don't mind…She called in at 4:15 on Friday afternoon to say she wouldn't be in until 7 o'clock that night. That was *after* I had left for the day and my staff person had already showed up for her shift."

I was puzzled. "What's the significance of that?"

"We ask our residents to call us before four o'clock so we'll know if we need to call in a staff member. In this case, this girl was the only resident that evening. We ended up paying a staff member to be there for nothing! This girl just doesn't show any respect, no matter how many chances we give her."

I noticed her use of the judgmental word "respect." "I see," I said, connecting the dots. "So you're able to have your staff person come in later if they're not needed?"

"That's right," she answered. "Our money is super tight and every dollar counts."

"Yes, I can imagine it is," I said.

I thought about her dilemma for a moment. She obviously needed her teen client to cooperate if she was going to get the most staffing out of the agency's limited budget.

"Let me ask you something," I offered. "Who is this issue all about? In other words, are you focused on *your* needs or *her* needs?"

She paused. "Well, I guess this issue is about our needs. We need the girls to tell us by noon, really, whether they'll be in or not so we can staff accordingly. Also, in this case, the extreme of staying out all night causes staff to worry. Following the curfews and returning when you state you will is the respectful thing to do."

"What do you mean by 'respectful'?" I asked, aware that this judgmental word was a plank in her eye.

"It means we want them to abide by a few simple rules because their actions affect others in the home." She waited, expecting me to readily agree with what she viewed as obvious common sense.

I didn't bite. Instead, I empathized. "I can understand why you would say that, Joan. You're providing a great service and just asking for a few rules to be followed!"

"That's right!" she exclaimed.

I went on. "I'm wondering whether your approach is getting you what you want with this young woman. By that I mean, your job as a leader is to influence her to behave the way you want her to behave. You're choosing to use a method that says, 'If you don't do it our way, you're out of here.' Is that fair to say?"

Joan answered quietly. "Yes, that is true I guess…" Suddenly her voice picked up energy. "But what else are we supposed to do? Be nice-nice all the time and let the residents walk all over us?" I had often heard this conundrum expressed by leaders, from executives to parents. She was merely expressing the hammer versus the doormat dilemma!

"There is another alternative. It's the basis of the leadership work that I do. What you do is identify the behavior you want to change and focus on what do you need to do to get that behavior to happen. I don't have enough detail from you to give you any specific advice, but that's the principle—find new choices that are neither nice-nice nor holding a gun to their head!" I went on. "Do you want to get specific about your situation?"

"Yes, I do actually. I don't feel good about this situation, but I'm at a loss as to what else I can do."

"Let's begin by me asking you some questions," I said. "Why does it matter that she tells you about her weekend plans by a certain time of the day?"

"So we can know how to staff the house. We need to know by twelve noon at the latest."

"Okay," I said. "Then that becomes your leadership goal. You're saying you want this girl to start telling you her weekend plans by Friday at noon. The key is to get her to willingly agree to do this. How do you think she is feeling about your current approach to getting her to give you her return time?"

"Not very good," Joan answered pensively.

"Is that what you want?"

"No."

"What do you want?"

"I want her to leave feeling good about her time with us, not feeling anxious to get out as soon as she can. But I am afraid that this is not how our clients feel. They already tell me that they want to get out of here as soon as they can. I guess they just want their independence," she murmured.

"Is that what you want? Girls who leaved feeling glad to get out of your home? You see Joan, you're at risk of succeeding in giving them a roof over their heads, but failing to give them the experience of *feeling* the love of Christ." I let that sink in for a moment.

"How important is that to you?" I asked her.

"Very!" Joan answered emphatically.

"Well, do you see how your approach may cause the very opposite of what you want?" I paused. "Do these girls have good self-esteem?"

"No-o. Their self-esteem is terrible."

"That's what I would have expected. You see, when a person's self-esteem is low, their self-image is, *I'm not lovable.* When you, as a Christian woman, begin to love this girl, you are causing dissonance within her—inner conflict at an unconscious level. She believes she is unlovable, yet here she is, getting all this love and support from you! This clashes within her and she thinks, *One of us must be wrong here—either I'm wrong and really am lovable, or they're wrong and just haven't seen the real, unlovable me yet.* So she begins to test you to see who is wrong. If you treat her like everyone else has treated her—negatively and critically whenever she is "bad," she unconsciously says to herself, *Ah-ha! Just as I suspected. I am unlovable! I did bad, and now I'm being judged and abandoned, just like always.* This is the problem with what I call traditional Hammer or Doormat leadership. She will link your consequence of asking her to leave to her own low self-worth. What you need to do is give her a *natural* consequence linked to her behavior, along with positive incentives, rather than relying on a punitive consequences to pressure her into changing."

I waited. It was a lot to dump onto my sweet, loving friend. I checked in with her. "Is this making sense?"

"Yes, it is making sense. I do feel afraid that I've set up a lose-lose situation by giving her that letter which we will have to act on, and which will then lead to this awful experience for her *and* for us."

"That's exactly the risk that you face. By writing this letter, you've made this an ego contest—a power play to see who is going to be the king of the hill."

"So what can I do now that the letter is already signed?" she asked. This was a moment of joy for me, because here was a leader ready to try to win differently—with the love of Jesus, without fear and control!

"There are always many ways to solve leadership challenges. However, in this case I suggest you eat humble pie," I said.

"Eat humble pie? What do you mean?" she asked quizzically.

"I mean, go and tell her that you were wrong to write that letter, tear it up and then lay your problem on her: that you can't afford to pay people when there is no need to have a staff person on duty. Ask her to solve it. Make sure you give her the big picture perspective by reminding her, 'We want to be helpful to you, yet we need to be very conservative with our money, because we don't have much. It's so important for us so that we'll have enough money to keep this place going for other girls too. You can help by giving me a timely notice about whether you'll be here or not.'"

"What you're doing with this approach," I added, "is connecting her to the 'purpose' of this agency. This is one of the four anchors in the leadership work I do. Then wait for her answer and go from there. Look for find ways to be helpful to her. For example, ask her if she needs a sticky note with the number written on it. Does she know where the phones are at her school?"

Joan sat on the phone in silence. I wondered if I gave her too much to digest. Suddenly, she broke out. "Can you do a workshop for our whole staff? We need to learn this approach! All of us are struggling with this and none of us want the girls to leave feeling they had a negative experience..."

"Sure," I said, feeling a glow of joy as I gave thanks to the work of the Holy Spirit, happening right in front of my eyes. *Thank you Lord, for the joy of this moment. I feel your love and I know your love just made a difference in someone else's life, who will in turn impact other lives.*

This is a classic leadership challenge—how to influence people without hammering them with the rule book. When a client or loved one fails to "respect" the rules, we often move from being nice-nice (Doormat) to using punitive consequences (Hammer) because these are the only two choices we have in our leadership tool bags.

Jesus shows us a different way. He begins with non-judgment, as He did with the adulterous woman and the woman at the well. Non-judgment removes the log from our eye so we can see clearly new ways in which to discern how to win what we want, with love. Once Joan stopped judging as "disrespectful," residents who did not call staff with their plans, she could begin to see alternative ways to cooperatively and lovingly win this young woman. Her goal shifted from "How can I get my way?" to "How can I influence this young woman to give me what I want in a way that will forever leave an imprint on her heart: the realization that the love of Jesus is *different* from the conditional, judgmental, manipulative love that is so abundant in this world."

Importantly, this does not mean that having a rule that results in "kicking out" someone you care about is sinful or wrong. In fact, making him or her aware of this consequence can be a good thing. It only means that this would be done as a last resort, and with love in your heart, not condemnation. Remember that non-judgment is the intention that lies in your heart, not the action you take. Your loved one is free to make his or her own choices. You will know your motives were judgmental if you are not at peace when they choose to live with the consequences, rather than make the choice you want them to make.

Our job as Christian leaders is to leave behind us the imprint of Jesus' love. We do this by the character of our actions and the joy in our hearts, not by the weight of our judgments or our punitive consequences. Jesus wrote in John 12:47, "As for the person who hears my words but does not keep them, I do not judge him. For I did not come to judge the world, but to save it." (NIV) Wise leaders focus on saving people with love, not shaming them with our approval and disapproval.

Group Study: Wisdom Lesson 4-4: Decide to intentionally influence someone's behavior. Use the Appendix at the back of this book. This nine-step WIN Leadership Goal-Setting Template will help you isolate who you want to influence, what you've been doing so far, and what the cost is of failing to effectively lead them. With this in hand, focus on step nine. What other ways could you help your loved one make real behavior changes? Be creative! Notice when they do it and praise them. Give small incentives. Simply ask them if they would mind doing what you want. Be ready to non-judgmentally accept their response, no matter what it may be. But don't give up either.

NOTES

_____

_____

_____

_____

_____

4-5 Simple Solutions: A Complaining Teenager

When you are non-judgmental, wisdom often just pops into your head in the form of inspirations. I don't believe this is a coincidence. In Psalm 46:10, God promises, "Be still and know that I am God." (NIV). God's spirit is alive in you, and when you are non-judgmental, you will hear His voice. Non-judgment leaves your mind ready to receive His Counsel, trust His quiet inner voice, and act on His guidance swiftly and surely. The following story depicts a simple, everyday incident that comprises the vast majority of judgmental conflicts in everyday family life. With a non-judgmental frame of mind, your family life will go more smoothly right in the present moment that a conflict is happening.

This is especially crucial for any parent who wants to teach his or her children to do new tasks competently and willingly. In the following situation, we are looking at a common household situation—clearing the table and the dirty dishes after dinner. This topic was the scene of many conflicts in our household when I was growing up!

Dad leaned back in his chair, letting Sunday evening dinner settle in his stomach. He looked over at his wife and smiled. She had prepared another wonderful meal. Then he looked at his two daughters, Sarah and Kelly aged twelve and fourteen.

"Would you girls mind clearing the table and the dirty dishes?" he asked.

"Sure," they responded easily. Sarah looked over at Kelly. "I set the table, so you have to clear it!"

"Yeah," responded Kelly, "but I set it the last two days!" After a brief argument, they began clearing dishes and putting them into the dishwasher.

As they cleared the dishes, Dad participated in putting the dishes away. His elder daughter Kelly peered into the partially loaded dishwasher and said, "There's no room to put in the plates." She looked up plaintively at him, hoping he would solve her problem as he had so often in the past.

"Really?" he asked, walking over to take a look. "Oh, I see what's wrong. The little plates are in the rack where the large plates go. I find that loading works best if you put the little ones either on the top rack or at the back here." He pointed to the back, letting her reach down to move the plates. She carefully used the very tips of her fingers. Getting her hands dirty was "icky" for her. She was at that age where her reaction to almost everything was, "Ugh-h!! That's DISGUSTING!!" and, "You are so-o ANNOYING!"

As the dishes were nearly done, Kelly attempted to quietly slip out of the kitchen. Dad noticed the table needed to be wiped and asked her to do it. Kelly rolled her eyes and reluctantly obeyed. Dad didn't say anything as he continued working with Sarah to get the last few dirty dishes into the dishwasher. When he looked up, he saw Kelly leaning over the now cleared kitchen table. She was delicately holding the corner of the wipe rag with the tips of her thumb and forefinger, lightly swishing the rag across the table. Crumbs were falling onto the floor and sticky residue was getting gently caressed, not scrubbed!

Normally, he would have felt that old familiar judgmental niggle, leading to some kind of sarcastic remark along with a command to cease and desist! This time, he felt at peace. The time he spent intentionally accepting that she was at that incredibly judgmental age of being a teenager was about to pay off.

"Honey, that approach isn't going to work," he offered.

"Well, I am *not* going to touch this rag," Kelly said with determination. "Do you *know* where it's been all day? Sitting in that yucky sink!"

Mom overheard the conversation and poked her head in to the kitchen. "Kelly! You will never get the table clean like that! Now stop being so silly and take that dishrag and hold it properly!"

Kelly wrinkled her face in disgust and hung her head. Dad focused on her for a moment. He knew Kelly despised getting her hands dirty. He had come to peace about that, even though his own mother would have never tolerated such nonsense.

"It is pretty yucky, isn't it," he said agreeably. Suddenly an idea popped into his head. "Kelly, would it be easier if you put on a rubber glove? That way you could scrub the table without getting your hands wet!"

Kelly brightened up. "Hey, that's a good idea. Sure!"

Dad reached under the sink and pulled out the glove. Mom smiled while Kelly proceeded to give the table a good scrubbing.

What leadership lesson can we learn from this typical, daily situation? First of all, it's important to note the process. The first step was to have a clear leadership goal: to train the girls in the task of properly setting up the dirty dishes in the dishwasher. Dad took the leadership role by asking the girls to do the job, as well as supportively training them on *how* to do the job. When the table-wiping incident arose, Dad was ready. By *already* being in a non-judgmental leadership frame of mind, he didn't get blinded by the typical "power play" move of trying to make his daughter do it Dad's way. Furthermore, he didn't get hooked by her judgmental comments, tone of voice and body language, all of which are typical emotional "hooks" that shift our focus away from the issue (wiping the table) and onto the judgment (getting your hands wet is disgusting).

Instead, Dad immediately found a way to meet Kelly's need for dry hands *and* get the job done. The whole incident happened in a few seconds. That is the main reward of being non-judgmental. The leader is able to see new choices *right in the moment*. Otherwise, this kind of incident could easily have blown into a major power struggle, if not between himself and Emily, then certainly between Emily and her mother. Let us remember Paul's words to parents: "**Fathers, do not provoke your children to anger, but bring them up with the training and instruction of the Lord."** (EPH 6:4 NAB)

The inability to get other people to change is a major cause of conflict and broken relationships. You will enjoy your life and make a Christ-like difference in the lives of your loved ones every day if you make it your daily prayer to eliminate your own judgmental desire to approve or disapprove of their behaviors, habits, and choices in life. Perhaps your wife almost never apologizes for her role in a conflict. If this bothers you, when she does, you will be apt to think, "It's about time you took some responsibility too!" That would be a thought of the "smart" variety that will make it very difficult for you to do the *wise* thing—to compliment and thank her for it. This is, of course, the very thing you need to do if you want her to apologize more often! If you continue to follow the path of judgment, your judgmental attitude will color your response, and she will learn that it is not safe to apologize to you.

Non-judgment will help you see new ways to influence your husband, wife, son, daughter or parent's behavior. First, however, you must become humble enough to change yourself—to see the way in which your own response is defeating the very behavior change you want from your loved one.

Group Study: Wisdom Lesson 4-5: Get over one annoying habit coming from someone who bothers you. Make a list of favorite phrases or habits that this person does. Maybe she complains about the lack of cupboard space over and over again. Maybe he has an irritating habit of falling asleep on the couch when guests come over. Perhaps your kids constantly push the limits of their bedtime or curfew time. Can you see the world through their eyes? How does it serve them to complain? Can you be at peace with the idea that they are free to continue with their annoying habit? Now can you see ways in which to help them transform their habit? Go back to the Stop, Start, Keep Doing lists in Lesson 4-3 for ideas.

NOTES

4-6 Overcome People Who Frustrate You: The Sleeping-In Teen

I was doing a leadership workshop. One of the students was Peter, an energetic father of two young women aged eighteen and twenty. Peter stood up to declare that what he wanted to change in his youngest daughter was her lack of respect. I asked him if he could "do" lack of respect. Right here. Right now. Naturally, he couldn't. Peter had slipped into a typical leadership fault. He was "labeling" his daughter's behavior as "disrespectful." Any word that describes a behavior as "good" or "bad" is a label. Every such label is a judgment.

I asked him to define the actual behavior that she was doing. He said, "She gets up at quarter to eight and expects a ride to school from me when I have to leave by eight o'clock." He went on, his annoyance rising by the second. "My other daughter and I often have to wait for her and it frustrates me to no end!"

"How long has this been going on?" I asked him.

"Nearly five years!" he exclaimed indignantly.

"Wow, that's a long time," I offered sympathetically. "What do you want her to do instead?"

"I want her to show some respect!" My earlier lesson about the difference between a judgmental label and the underlying behavior obviously hadn't sunk in yet.

"Okay," I responded, "you want respect. What does that look like in behavior?"

After several tries, he offered a specific behavior. "I want her to get up by at least seven o'clock or even seven-thirty."

"Excellent!" I said. "Now you've identified your leadership goal. You know what behavior you want from her, and if you get it, you'll know you have succeeded!" He smiled nervously at that inconceivable thought.

I began to question the rest of the group about what Peter could do to intentionally influence his daughter. One person suggested he leave on time without her. This would be giving her a natural consequence—normally an excellent leadership tool.

"Done that," he said flatly. "It didn't work."

"Why not? I asked.

"My wife will then take her to school, or she just takes a taxi."

"Ah-h," I said. "So there's a leak in the parental boat." Everyone laughed.

"Does she take the taxi with her own money?" I queried.

"Yes, but she just comes back to me later for more money anyway." Obviously, he was contributing to his own demise. I chose not to mention that just yet.

Peter was clearly losing a classic power struggle with his daughter and getting no support from his wife. He was at his wit's end about what to do. It occurred to me that getting his wife onside might be the first place he should go, rather than battling on alone. I decided not to get sidetracked by that dangling carrot. Changing his wife's behavior is an entirely different leadership goal!

Peter looked over at me. "I know you said leaders go from using the hammer to being a doormat. Well, I've tried both. I've tried taking her alarm clock and moving it out of reach so she *has* to get out of bed. I've even tried spraying water right in her face when it's time to get up." A chuckle went through the room.

"What happened when you tried those techniques?" I asked.

"They worked but only that one time. As soon as I stopped doing it, she went right back to sleeping in. Nothing I do motivates her to stop! So I've become a doormat. I admit it! I keep hoping if I'm just patient enough, she'll grow out of this."

I smiled. This is the common dilemma for many parents and business leaders who get pushed to their emotional limits. They become afraid of what they might do if they really use the Hammer. Most men in particular have some measure of rage buried somewhere that could be triggered under the right circumstances. That's why so many men switch to being Doormats if the Hammer fails. It often feels better than risking a fury of rage that could get out of control. Losing control is what makes connecting with your feelings so frightening. *What if I lose it?* you ask yourself.

Earlier, Peter had made clear that he wasn't just trying to get himself out of the house on time. He was also gravely concerned that his daughter might develop a life-long lazy streak that would impede her ability to keep a job. Peter was a perfect example of a well-intentioned father who was letting the past and the future cloud his present-moment leadership skills. His five years of pent-up frustration (the past) was oozing out of his every pore. His future-based fears of his daughter sitting on unemployment, perhaps living with him and his wife well into their retirement years and being a financial burden on him all rolled into the present moment to cloud his ability to make new, wiser choices.

For Peter, winning this battle was a matter of respect. He especially contrasted his eighteen year old's tardiness with his twenty-year old daughter's marvelous habits of organization and timeliness. Could this be part of their emotional drama? In all likelihood it was, with his younger daughter resisting his every effort to pressure her into *making* her be like "Miss Perfect big sister."

Someone in the group suggested that his vigorous reaction to her tardiness was probably feeding her. I jumped in. "I suspect that is very true in this case, Peter. Your response to your daughter's tardiness is giving her a payoff that works for her. Perhaps it is that she knows she can 'pull your chain,' and that gives her a feeling of power. Perhaps this is part of her lifelong way of getting attention from you. Who knows? And who cares really? What matters, is that you need to focus on what can you do now to break this vicious cycle that is clearly causing you enormous grief!" His shoulders sagged with relief at that thought.

I wanted Peter to consider the W.I.N. principle as the basis for solving this problem. I began by asking him a question designed to help him clarify his boundaries between himself and his now adult daughter. "Whose space is it to decide what her morning wake-up routine is?" Peter thought for a moment. Then he grimaced and said, "Her space."

"I agree. Whose space is involved when you consider the issue of leaving on time."

"My space," he said without hesitation.

"Terrific," I said. "So what is yours to *resist* and hers for you to *support?*"

"I get it," he said, his eyes brightening up. "But still, how do I get her to be ready on time?"

"You've got a number of options," I suggested. "You can leave on time regardless. If your wife takes her to school, isn't that her right and privilege? You are getting away on time and that is your space."

He came right back at me. "But what about my concern for her developing long term habits that she'll need to get and keep a job. She just doesn't seem to care…" his voice trailed off. As I often find, the surface motive is usually just that. In reality, she was triggering deeper fears in him. He was projecting his beliefs onto her, beliefs such as "people who sleep in are lazy and can't keep a job."

"She's eighteen," I countered. "She's not worried about jobs, and what her current habits mean for her career ten years from now. She's thinking about *now!*

If you want to influence her, you've got to see her through her own eyes, not your eyes."

"Well, she will get up early if her friend comes over to have a smoke with her. Then she's up at seven o'clock, no problem!"

"And what do you do when she gets up like that?" I asked openly. "Do you give her any praise or recognition?"

"Are you kidding?" He looked incredulously at me. "She's out there *smoking*! I'm not going to endorse that!" His judgments about her smoking were clearly evident in his tone of voice. Once again, judgments were blinding him from doing what's important now. She was demonstrating the very behavior he wanted, and instead of rewarding her, he held his nose! As a leader, you can't turn a sow's ear into a silk purse in one shot. You take what they give you and you work with it! Ignore the smoking. Praise her early rising. It is her "space" to decide whether to smoke or not. Disapproving of her smoking habit is merely blinding you from helping her learn to get up earlier. Good leaders keep their eyes on the prize! Her smoking is irrelevant for now. In addition, judging her smoking won't influence her to quit either—any smoker can tell you that.

When you support other people—their right to make their own decisions about issues that are theirs to decide—you build trust. This requires humility, which is a key ingredient in effective leadership. Peter had turned this into an ego-based power struggle. His daughter clearly intended to match him, blow for blow. By supporting her right to sleep in, he would be saying, I accept you as you are. He is *not* saying, I agree with sleeping in late. He is simply ending his judgments about those behaviors. Now he will be able to see what's important for him to do to intentionally influence his daughter to *help* her change those behaviors.

I left him with some actions to consider. First, as always, he has to focus on being non-judgmental about her behavior. He can ask himself, *How can I accept the possibility that my daughter will never change and that I will never be able to do anything to force her to change?* God is in control of her, not you.

Second, resist where it is his space to resist. Leave on time, no matter what. If his wife wants to drive her daughter every day, she has that freedom. Many mothers are "rescuers" of their children, as are fathers, and trying to influence that behavior is an entirely separate leadership challenge! Hopefully, mother will also tire of the burden of driving her daughter on a daily basis. The main point here is that Peter must end the emotional drama, and that starts by getting non-judgmental about her behavior. He must also model the behavior he wants her to emulate, namely, that successful people leave on time. He must not let her tardiness derail him from doing the right thing for him.

Third, he must explore ways to support his daughter's choice—the opposite of what he had done up until till then. He could consider preparing her breakfast in advance so she could be ready more quickly in the fifteen minutes she allows herself to get ready. He could look for other ways to say, "*I love you just the way you are…*AND I will be true to my own needs." This way, he will avoid resentfully rescuing her while feeling that he *had* to be late in order to wait for her. She cannot *make* him be late. He always has a choice. The question is, can he do what feels right for him without feeling guilty, mean or that he is a "bad" father?

Other ideas for Peter to consider are to make the problem hers, but not the solution. The problem is her inability to get ready on time. His solution is for her to get up earlier. She may indeed have ideas for different solutions. Accept any solution that helps the cause. Another leadership tool for him is recognizing her when she *does* show up on time. "Have you ever done that before?" I asked Peter.

"No!" he said. "I *expect* her to get up early. I'm not going to reward something she should already be doing!"

This is a major mistake commonly made by many leaders. If you want more of a certain behavior, you must water the seed. Reward it when it happens in a meaningful way. He could even encourage the behavior with temporary incentives by giving her something she values if she is ready on time, such as movie tickets or use of the car. The key to this kind of non-judgmental leadership is to reduce and eventually withdraw the rewards as soon as she is on track for a time. As a leader, you want her to do it for her own reasons, freely and willingly. The incentive is merely a "kickstarter," and must not be allowed to remain as the ongoing reason for her to carry out a new behavior.

Sometimes, parents feel guilty about using these techniques. Some of them feel like "tough love." Indeed, they are tough love—to resist means taking away choices they want from you, like waiting on them. They want you to cave in on what is your space. You will be tough more easily when you reframe your beliefs to be non-judgmental. If Dad is doing God's will here, and doing God's will means leaving by eight o'clock, what is there to feel guilty about? Jesus said, "**For** whoever does the will of my heavenly Father is my brother, and sister, and mother." (MT 12:50 NAB) This is part of obeying the greatest law—to love God with all your heart, mind, body and soul.

As parents, we must always seek to be clear about our own intentions. Peter's intentions began with, "I want her to wake up by 7:15 A.M." This is trying to control her space. With some reflection and clarification, his intention shifted to "I want to leave by 8 o'clock and have her ready to go with me at that time." This shift in intention is so simple. Yet for most of us, we are blinded by our own judgments and labels. We get hooked into a battle of solutions, rather than inviting our loved one to find their own solutions to their own problems. Your role is to provide consistent boundaries (resist) while helping them make real behavior changes (support)—changes they probably agree with in the first place if they are honest with themselves.

Group Study: Wisdom Lesson 4-6: Can you support someone whose behavior you totally disagree with? Imagine a pregnant young woman came to you determined to have an abortion. What would you do? Could you stand by her side? Could you drive her to the clinic and then pick her up afterwards? How far should a person go to show support for other people's unwise choices? Explore the same question using cigarettes in the above example. Would it be reasonable for Peter to offer his daughter cigarettes as an incentive to be ready on time for work? Consider how Jesus dined with tax collectors. What did he do such that they freely and willingly changed their cheating ways? See Luke 19:1-10.

NOTES

Lesson 5

YOU ARE PURPOSEFUL, NOT SUCCESSFUL

A man who runs a cancer hospice in San Francisco appeared on the Oprah Winfrey television show. He had seen over three hundred people face their last days on this earth. Oprah asked him what these people thought about during their final days. He said they asked themselves just two questions:

1. Was I loved?
2. Did I love well?

If these are the last two questions people who are dying ask, is it fair to conclude that *love* is the purpose of life? Jesus says it is. He said that the two greatest commands are to love God and to love one another as we love ourselves. (Mt 22:37-40) Jesus came to earth with just one purpose—to show us what love looks like, sounds like and acts like. His death and resurrection are the ultimate act of love, not because of his horrible suffering, but because of his complete innocence on our behalf.

This chapter will help you stay true to God's purpose for your life in the face of judgments from others and judgments that you inflict upon yourself: self-judgment. In a secular sense, this is often expressed as "To thine own self, be true." In a Christian sense, we say, "Thy Will be done." Outwardly, both appear to describe the same thing—a person who marches to the beat of his or her own drummer. Inwardly, the reasons underlying each statement are completely different. The former elevates the individual. The latter asserts the importance of doing God's will, even at the expense of yourself or the approval of others. The Pharisees recognized this quality in Jesus: "'Teacher,' they said, 'we know that you are a man of integrity and that you teach the way of God in accordance with the truth. You aren't swayed by men, because you pay no attention to who they are." (MT 22:16 NIV) Jesus was like a soldier in the military. He obeyed the will of God, no matter what the price. When you are non-judgmental, you stop trying to control what others do, and focus on the discipline of doing His will as your highest priority.

You will trust that what is happening in the present moment serves His purpose for you. Your only job is to discern His will for you and to carry it out, even if this means that you will not be successful in a worldly sense.

Jesus captured his purpose on earth clearly in John 12:47 (NIV): "As for the person who hears my words but does not keep them, I do not judge him. For I did not come to judge the world but to save it." How did Jesus save the world? By loving us to the point of laying down his life for us, his flock. Do you think his family and friends *liked* this? We know they didn't, as we see from the incident in which Peter tried to "save" Jesus from his destiny on the cross. Do you think Jesus liked this himself? He prayed on the night before he died, "Father, if you are willing, take this cup from me; yet not my will but yours be done." (LK 22:42 NIV) Your loved ones, friends and colleagues may feel hurt by your actions as you pursue God's purpose for your life. Your challenge is to help them through these trials, while not being swayed by their approval or disapproval of what you should be doing with your life.

Non-judgment is central to achieving your purpose in life because if you don't like the cup the Father is giving you, you will become judgmental about it. You will say, *"Why me? Why aren't things going my way? Why is my marriage such a struggle? Why is my business failing? Why can't I get the job I want?"* When you look for answers by asking "why," you will find your judgments—the ways in which you feel persecuted by someone who is at fault for your unhappy circumstances. Perhaps you will blame other people who close doors, refuse to help you or don't return your phone calls. Perhaps you will blame yourself because you are not smart enough, skilled enough, rich enough or attractive enough. Perhaps you will blame God Himself, asking why He is not blessing you with success. You might blame Him for not meeting your expectations that as a believer, you deserve rewards of some kind.

God loves you. Whatever trials He is allowing in your life have that one purpose in mind—to teach you how to be fully dependent on His love, which is sufficient for all your needs. James crystallizes this when he writes, "Blessed is the man who perseveres under trial, because when he has stood the test, he will receive the crown of life that God has promised to those who love him." (JA 1:12 NIV) You will achieve your purpose when you live as if you have nothing to hide, nothing to prove and nothing to lose. When you have no attachments to this world, you have everything—God's love.

Does this sound idyllic? Pie in the sky? Nice to read about in the Bible but no one really does it? I do believe that you would be right to think that. My dearly departed Bible study brother, Ed Sharpe, once said to me, "The only tragedy about Mother Teresa is that she stands out so much." His point was that there ought to be a million Mother Teresa's. That, however, is not your problem. That is God's problem. Your problem is to fulfill God's purpose for your life. You must let go of forcing your life to be the way you once believed it ought to be.

James pointed this out in James 4:13-16: "Now listen, you who say, 'Today or tomorrow we will go to this or that city, spend a year there, carry on business and make money.' Why you do not even know what will happen tomorrow. What is your life? You are a mist that appears for a little while and then vanishes. Instead, you ought to say, 'If it is the Lord's will, we will live and do this or that.' As it is, you boast and brag. All such boasting is evil. Anyone, then, who knows the good he ought to do and doesn't do it, sins." (NIV)

As you become more non-judgmental, you become more present-moment focused. The present moment is where God is, the source of love. God is eternal and so is the present moment. You can only be present-moment focused if you face the moment as it really it is, without comparing it to your future expectations or past experiences. You must accept it, and then discern His will. This will cause you to be increasingly dependent on God for everything in your life. You will truly live with this credo: "Rejoice always. Pray without ceasing. In all circumstances give thanks, for this is the will of God for you in Christ Jesus." (1TH 5:16-18 NAB)

You will feel the presence of the Holy Spirit in your life every day, all day, and unleash the grace and joy of the Holy Spirit in your life. As you answer his call, you will want to do His will, even if others disagree with you. You will live as Jesus asked us: "Anyone who loves his father or mother more than me is not worthy of me; anyone who loves his son or daughter more than me is not worthy of me; and anyone who does not take his cross and follow me is not worthy of me." (MT 10:37-38 NIV)

Doing the will of God is frightening. The following story will show you how the fear of being judged gets in the way of believing men who are reluctant to even *think* about God during the course of their day, let alone openly and actively express their faith in their day to day lives.

5-1 Fear of Rejection: Thinking about God All Day Long

A group of men were gathered in His name at a Bible study. The question arose about why we spend so little time thinking about God during our day to day lives.

"I'm too busy thinking about the next three things I have to do," said Bob.

"I don't know why I don't," said Sam. "I have a few minutes throughout my day where I could think about God...I just don't! I guess I'm just focused on doing my work."

I laid back and listened to the various comments. I could feel some energy rising as the men began to offer solutions in our struggle to keep God front and center in our lives.

"I know one pastor who sets his watch to ring an alarm every twenty minutes," offered Jack, "just to remind himself to think about God."

"I think we just have to keep pulling ourselves back to center," said Pete. "We wander off the track and just need to try harder. It's like we need a rubber band to keep pulling us back on track!" He smiled at the thought. Several men nodded in agreement.

I spoke up with some passion. "You know, I must confess that I feel like I have heard this 'let's try harder' solution many times in my life. Have you guys heard that one before?" Several nodded in agreement. "Let me ask you something," I said. "Has it worked?" I waited for their answer. The silence was loud. After a several long seconds, I went on, "If 'trying harder' hasn't worked before, what are the odds that it will work this time?"

"Pretty low," said one man.

"I agree," I responded. Then I challenged them. "I have a different approach to dealing with this one, and it means actually looking at our shortcomings and the things we'd rather do than focus on God. Would you be willing to spend some time on this?"

After the usual quietness, they agreed this would be good and useful.

I began. "Why do you think you don't think about God regularly and frequently during your day?"

Bob spoke right up. "I'm too busy thinking about the next three things I have to do."

Sam echoed his sentiment. "Yeah. I've got a dozen things on my mind all day, trying to get the job done."

"Okay," I said, "You're busy thinking about the many things you have to do. I can certainly understand that. What do you think would happen if you stopped thinking about your work list all day?"

"Well," replied Bob, "I'd forget something. Then the job would get messed up. I'd end up with a very unhappy customer, or cost myself a whole bunch of money."

Sam agreed. "I have so many things I have to keep track of. If I was thinking about God, I'd forget something for sure!"

One of my greatest joys has been the discovery that we find our own truth when we look at what might go wrong, straight in the eye, rather than veering away from it. So I responded: "So let's say that happens, and you *do* forget something, and things *do* go sideways. What would be wrong with that?"

"Well, c'mon! Business is tough enough without making mistakes, getting customers upset and all that!" The group looked at me a bit warily, like, *Where is this guy going with this?*

"Why do you think that thinking about God will cause these disasters to happen?"

Jack piped up. "Because we won't be paying attention. We'll have our mind on Him, rather than on our work."

"What else might happen if you had your mind on God all day?" They considered my question. Sam spoke up. "We might start speaking about Him."

"How do you feel about that possibility?" I asked.

He paused. "People often don't like to hear about God. They get mad, or they just don't call back and you lose the business. You could even lose some friends."

"Yeah," said Jack who had been listening quietly. "You want to get along with the guys you work with. I know it's not right...but it's true, we want to be accepted." he said, his voice trailing off.

I played the conversation back to them. "So thinking about God could lead to speaking about God, which could lead to losing business, or getting rejected by the people you work with?"

"Yes, that's right," said Sam. "It's so hard, isn't it? Here we are, committed believers, and we're reluctant to even *think* about God for fear of what other people will do."

When you are purposeful in a Godly way, God is at the front and center of your life, overriding your work, your spouse, children, friends and family. When He is, you will feel His peace every day, just as Jesus promised. Your doubts and anxiety will begin to fade as you learn day by day that He is faithful *especially* when you are faithful. I find that as my faith has deepened, God is with me in whatever I am doing. I am having a constant dialogue with him, asking him things like, *"What I should do next, Lord?" "Why are you giving me this obstacle Lord?"* I am also conversing with Him, saying, *"What a beautiful sky you are giving us right now!" "Forgive me Father, I am struggling right now with this person. What should I do?"* God is your ever-present Father whose only goal is to *help* you succeed. Your challenge is to find His purpose that is hidden in your struggle.

The fear that others will reject us because of our faith is the barrier to living a purposeful life. The experience I have had is that some of your fears will come true but most won't. There will be those who are threatened by your open expression of your faith in God. They may let you know by ridiculing your faith. "What do you mean, 'God' is helping you?" they snort! "God isn't doing it. *You're* doing it! You've got to make your own breaks in this world, pal. Don't go blaming God for everything that happens in your life!" With compassion, you can now handle this sort of criticism. Maybe they will grow silent and remain distant from you. Sometimes they won't return your phone calls and drop their relationship with you. Take comfort in these words from Jesus, "Everyone who acknowledges me before others I will acknowledge before my heavenly Father. But whoever denies me before others, I will deny before my heavenly Father." (MT 10:32-33 NAB)

A tougher situation you may face is when following God's will threatens your financial security. If your husband or wife is focused on financial security, your expression of following God's will may not cut it for them. They may begin to pressure you to "Get a real job", or say, "Maybe this isn't really God's will. You're just being stubborn!" If the pressure gets very heavy, you may hear them say, "You're being irresponsible. Your job is to provide for this family, not force us to sell our house and live in some basement apartment!"

There is only one answer you can rely on in these circumstances. You must discern God's will for you at that moment in time. I veered off His track about a year ago, yielding to my own stressed-out need to make more money *now*, urged along by my wife's understandable anxiety. I decided I would get a job as a car salesman. I calculated that would give me some flexibility in my time, let me use my business skills, and allow me to keep building my speaking and training career on the side. In no time, I got myself in front of two car dealers, one of whom owned eight dealerships. When I was done, I knew one thing. It would take me a year to build up a clientele and earn real money—the same year that I could spend doing the same thing building up a clientele for my own practice. Even more importantly, my peace was gone. I felt anxious and unsettled. After two weeks, I knew in my heart that I could not do it, even though my wife desperately wanted me to take any job in order to give her financial peace of mind. She left me two weeks later for the second time, and for what looked certain to be permanently. The story of how God worked His love into our lives from that second separation follows in the next section.

Every believer who wants to live a purposeful life, filled with meaning and leaving loveprints on those around him or her, must face the core fears in his or her life. Not having enough money is one core fear. Being rejected and abandoned by those he or she loves is another core fear.

Group Study: Purposeful Lesson 5-1: List common situations when you are tempted to speak about the Lord but don't. Is it saying a prayer out loud in a restaurant? Is it in explaining to a customer why you feel so happy today? Are you reluctant to name the Lord as the reason why things are the way they are in your life? List the judgments others might hold against you for your faith. Explore whether you could accept the possibility of these happening anyway. Identify one area where you might dare to do it and allow yourself see what happens next.

NOTES

5-2 True to God's Will: You Won't Change So She Leaves

The blessing that the Lord has given me in getting married twice is that you learn the most when you are in the most difficult of circumstances. In this way, I was blessed to learn in the first three years of my second marriage lessons that I see many couples struggling with twenty, thirty and even fifty years into their marriages. I don't say this to suggest that I have all the answers or that my second marriage is perfect. I say this to suggest that I have learned how to conquer the horrible dilemma of being true to your Godly purpose on this earth while helping an unbelieving wife deal with the very real side-effects of this commitment on her.

My wife left me for the second time during the third year of our marriage. I had learned how to accept her need for space, and to be thankful along the way. About ten months after she and I reconciled our marriage the first time around, a new set of tremors set in for me. I was struggling financially and she wanted me to give up building my leadership coaching and training practice and get a job with a steady income. She was frustrated and scared by our rapidly diminishing savings. When I resisted, she dealt with it by growing increasingly distant.

I began to be bothered by the distance in our relationship. I couldn't seem to shake it and so I knew that the unnerving time had come when I had to be real, not nice. God was telling me that it was time for me to lead, rather than merely "get out of the way," which had been my main approach all year long. I began to speak up in May. I said to her, "We are like two people rafting down the river of life in our own boats, both doing our own thing."

The issue became one of a power struggle. Whose boat shall we get into? I saw myself as already being in the marriage boat, but rowing alone. She saw me as doing my career my way and she felt I was not respecting her need for financial security. I felt she was not supportive of my work which I deeply believe is God's calling for my life. I began to say to her, "You don't get a vote if you're not in the boat."

The core issue here begins with boundaries. Whose space is it to decide what kind of work your partner does? I believe it is her space if it is her work, and your space if it is your work. This is a core foundation that must be addressed in your marriage if you are to be purposeful. Having said that, you are responsible for providing a living for your family, and I am totally committed to that too. How wealthy that living is, is a different matter, and therein lay the basis for much conflict and unhappiness.

Your partner is directly and personally affected by the choices you make, just as you are by her choices. The key to a healthy marriage is to accept the package your partner brings. The way you accept the package is by getting into the same boat. If she is hurting, you are affected. If you are hurting, she is affected. Your marriage is more important than money or your own comfort. It is not, however, more important than doing God's will for your life. There is room for both. Your personal challenge is to accept God's will for her life, and *her* personal challenge is to accept His will for *your* life. Neither is likely to include a guaranteed house size or annual vacation plan. Your spiritual challenge is to help each other accept this when one of you is making major and risky career choices.

In my case, I looked at career options that could improve our financial situation while keeping my work alive. When I no longer felt His peace, I knew that was not for me. She did not take the news well. I also began to express my unhappiness with the distant relationship we had developed over the previous months. Finally, the day came when a moment of truth arrived.

I said to her, "I want you to get in this boat with me. I don't know where it will go, but I want you to get in, and to ride it with me to the end, no matter what. If you decide you can't do that, I will understand. But until you do, I will continue to do my work my way." She said she would think about it. I felt renewed and rejuvenated, as I usually do when I finally face the real issue head on. The very next night she was curiously absent all day and well into the evening. She arrived around eleven P.M. She sounded very confident...too confident.

"I've thought it over what you said and I've decided that this marriage just isn't working. I'm moving out as of now."

I was stunned. The pit in my stomach reached new lows and I felt a crushing sensation. I didn't argue. With very few more words, she left.

The next day, I felt determined. This time it was over. I began digesting the idea that I was going to be a twice-divorced man who spoke about "the joys of being present and true to God's will and then you will feel His peace." What an awful feeling! My thoughts turned to God. "*So how is this supposed to be good for me, God?*" He didn't send me an email in response. I looked to the Bible and leaned with resignation on the scripture that says, "If the unbeliever separates, however, let him separate. The brother or sister is not bound in such cases; God has called you to peace." (1 COR 7:15 NAB)

Then came the crushing consequences. I cried when I broke the news to my son. He sat stunned, a blank look on his innocent seven year old face. He was losing his best friend in the whole world in his eight year old step-brother. He loved his step-sisters, and his step-mom too. He cried when he realized we wouldn't be going to Grandpa's on the east coast anymore. No more family traveling. No more driving around the fields in grandpa's ATV four wheeler. My heart lay busted on the floor. I had failed my son. Still, I drew strength from the fact that somehow God would turn this into something good. Somehow my faith in that remained unshakable.

A few days later, I spoke to the men in my bible study group, men whom I had known and studied with for four years. They were shocked and saddened at the news. I asked for their spiritual guidance, saying I did not intend to chase her this time. Indeed, I said, "I intend to lock the door behind her and get on with my life!" One of the guys stopped me dead in my tracks.

"Whoa, hold on a minute, John," he said gently but firmly. "You can let her go, but that doesn't mean you are not to accept her back if she wants to come back."

I looked at him with surprise. "What do you mean? You mean if she comes knocking on my door, I'm to take her back?"

"That's right," he came back. The other guys agreed. We looked up the passage: "To the rest I say (not the Lord): if any brother has a wife who is an unbeliever, and she is willing to go on living with him, he should not divorce her." (1 COR 7:12 NAB)

My heart was instantly changed by that powerful moment of spiritual truth. I realized that nothing had changed for me about her or what I wanted in our relationship. Thanks to my Christian brother, I narrowly escaped the grave danger of *reacting* to her leaving, rather than being purposeful. My purpose was to get her to join me in the marriage boat, for better or for worse. That remained unchanged. God was telling me that I was to leave my front door *wide open* for her, not slam it shut in angry retribution for leaving me.

I decided to call her, and she was surprisingly warm-hearted. She announced she had found herself a rental property and had signed the lease. She and the kids would be moving back to live near her ex-husband. She wanted to give me a chance to say good-bye to the children. I wanted that too. I had no intention of selling her on coming back and I made no effort to do so. I only knew my purpose had changed back one hundred and eighty degrees—to leave the door open for her to return to our marriage boat, just as I had before we separated.

Friday afternoon arrived, just nine days after our separation. We met at a park. I felt shaky. My heart was broken over the kids, especially my stepson Andrew. I felt shaky and emotional. Jared and I arrived first. Joanne pulled up shortly afterwards and we hugged each other along with each of the kids. Then we wandered over to the playground. After faking it for a few minutes by throwing a ball around, I asked her to hang back so I could speak to her children on my own.

I started with the girls, who were eleven and nearly thirteen. Joanne had told me that they were very upset about losing our house and having to change schools again.

"I'm very sad," I told them. "This is not what I want, but this is the way it is right now." My voice was full of emotion, but I kept it together. "How are you feeling?" I asked.

"I'm sad too," said Caroline, her warm eyes beaming up. "Me too," said Gen in her usual somewhat shy manner.

"I just want you to know something," I said. "What saddens me the most is how this will affect your idea of marriage someday. I want you to know that three people in your life have all made huge mistakes here and none of us is doing it right."

"Three?" said Caroline.

"Yes, three. Your mom is wrong to leave this marriage. Your dad was wrong the first time to leave her. And I was wrong to leave Jared's mom."

"Oh," she said, "I didn't think about you and Jared's mom…"

"Yes, I have made this same mistake and I know from experience that leaving your husband or wife doesn't fix your problems…" I paused. "So don't use us as your role models, okay?" I reached over to them. "I love you and I will miss you terribly."

"I love you too," said Caroline. "Me too," said Gen in her quiet way.

We chatted and made small talk for a few moments. Then I stood up to find Andrew. I called him over and we went over to the other side of the playground set, beside the slide. I couldn't speak. I just began to cry and cry and cry. Deep, racking, sobbing cries, on and on and on. I muffled the noise as best as I could, so as not to attract Joanne's attention. Andrew sat quietly beside me.

I finally spoke. "Is it okay if I cry?"

"Yeah, it's okay," he answered quietly.

"I think so too," I said. "I hope you never forget that for yourself Andrew. It's always okay to cry." I thought briefly of my own foolish twenty-five year stretch of never crying after the age of thirteen.

"You've been like a son to me, Andrew, and a fantastic brother to Jared. I'm going to miss you terribly," I said.

"I'll miss you too John," he answered quietly, looking me in the eye. I was impressed with how solid he was in the face of all my emotions.

"I love you Andrew," I said.

"I love you too."

"Can I give you a hug?" I asked.

"Yeah, sure." I reached over and he leaned into me. We hugged hard and long. A part of my soul felt like it died in that moment.

I began to cry again, my body weak and drained. Suddenly, she touched me. I looked up, somewhat surprised that I hadn't heard her come over. I steeled myself. I didn't want to be rescued nor have her pity. To my delight, she did neither. Quiet tears streamed down her face. I spoke first.

"I might as well tell you what I was going to tell you tomorrow."

"What's that?" she asked.

"I just want you to know that if you happen to get hit by a bolt of lightning and want to come back, my door remains open."

She looked up at me with surprise in her eyes. "I have to be honest," she said. "I haven't felt good about leaving you. It's been really eating at me these last days. I don't feel like I really lived up to my promises from last summer and given us a real chance."

I leaned on the post just to steady myself. Was I hearing what I thought I was hearing?

She went on. "I do want to come over tomorrow and talk about our relationship, if you'll still have me over."

I was in shock. Really? Then a doubtful voice creeped in. Where will the rollercoaster go next? I quickly squashed that voice. A miracle was happening right in front of my eyes. God is in charge.

We reconciled the next day. Then we took a week to work out what the boat would look like. She wasn't ready to jump in just like that. God works in wondrous ways, however, and an angel appeared in the form of a woman who was aware of our separation. We had gotten to know her and her husband through dinner with some other friends. This woman unexpectedly sent us a note, along with a book called Sleeping with Bread. This is the important part of what she wrote:

> *Dear John & Joanne,*
> *You have both been on my mind a lot and I hope it will not seem intrusive when I tell you I have been praying for "the best outcome" for you. Personally, I have found marriage difficult. I did not fully commit to ours until we attended a "Marriage Encounter" weekend. We had been married 22 years!*
> *...No one can really advise others about their lives. I believe you are both fine people who will be respectful of each other and caring towards your children as you find the right path for your lives.*
> *Shalom.*

This note had quite a profound impact on both of us. Joanne felt loved and supported as she saw that perhaps her inability to fully commit to our marriage after just three years wasn't so bad after all. I, too, saw with new eyes that I was asking Joanne for a huge leap of faith in a very short period of time. This softened my heart and strengthened my resolve that we both needed to be fully committed no matter what, for better and for worse.

We went camping for the weekend, and spent a rainy three hours in the back of our van talking about work and career. She wanted promises. I couldn't make any. "I'm on God's program. Wherever He takes me, that's where I'll go." I was asking for a complete leap of faith on her part. I could totally understand if she decided she just couldn't go there. It was a tumultuous, emotional day as she argued, cried and wrestled with the reality of our financial uncertainty, including the possibility of having to sell our house if we couldn't meet our mortgage payments. Oh, how she wanted me to just promise that would not happen! I could not make that promise.

Three hours later, she was still on the fence. We were just ten minutes from home when I said, "Do you plan to call the kids?" This was our cue. We had not yet told the kids the good news of our reconciliation. This became the point of no return in deciding one way or the other, once and for all. She felt this as pressure from me. She asked, "Are you saying that you are calling it quits if I don't fully commit?" Her undertone felt unsafe to me, like suddenly I was the one breaking up our marriage. I steadied myself.

"No," I said. "I'm giving you an invitation and you're either accepting it or rejecting it. You are free to decide whatever you want."

"Oh," she said, giving me that "it's all pretty plain to see" kind of look.

We pulled into our driveway moments later. As we unloaded our gear, I took her over to the stack of hay in our small barn. I love hay. The smell of hay makes me a kid again. She looked at me, and we faced and held each other. She asked just one question. "Can I trust you?"

I looked deep into her eyes and said, "Joanne, I love you and I promise to honor you and do my very best to provide a good life for all of us. That's all I can promise. Will you join me in our marriage boat, no matter what?"

She looked at me. "Yes, I will John. I will stay with you no matter what, for better or for worse, till death do us part." We leaped and we kissed and we hugged.

I knew in that moment that our marriage had found bedrock. Amen, Lord. Your grace alone saved our marriage. The journey of our lifetime had begun, with many chapters yet to be written, God willing.

Your wife needs to know you are there for life, no matter what. She also needs to know that you will carry out God's purpose for your life, no matter what. Furthermore, she needs to know you will support God's purpose for *her* life, no matter what. What is true for the husband is just as true for the wife. You must *both* trust that God will not put your Godly purposes at odds with each other. This is so much easier when you have a believing spouse, but remains even more important if you don't! When you are unequally yoked, your values will differ. Your ability to stay true to God's purpose while allowing her the freedom to be herself is the most powerful action you can take to help your spouse accept the Lord Jesus. Even with that, we must remember that it is the Holy Spirit who saves, and not us.

As a man, your conviction and integrity will provide the spiritual security your wife needs, far more than the financial security she *thinks* she needs. She will face financial uncertainty with confidence if you yourself are able to face it with confidence. The key is to not compromise on your core purpose for your life. Jesus did not compromise on his Godly purpose ever, in spite of enormous pressure and death threats. Your own fretting and worrying about your success will aggravate her insecurity. Your calmness and clarity that you will work hard and faithfully to carry out God's will, *and* that God will provide the money you need, is Christ-like leadership. Jesus did not promise his followers an easy life in worldly terms. Indeed, he promised them the opposite. Your job as a leader in Christ in your family is to be a rock of firmness in pursuit of your purpose, even if you are not successful in worldly terms.

Group Study: Purposeful Lesson 5-2: List the core values that bind your relationship with your spouse. Your list should be short, memorable and alive every day of your lives. Here are some examples to get you started:

We ask a lot and we give a lot.
We live a simple life.
We pray together.
We meet conflicts head on and do not avoid them.
We put God ahead of us.
We put us ahead of kids.
We put loved ones ahead of work.
We support each other, even if we disagree with each other.
We are on the same team, and are never enemies.
We assume the best and not the worst.

NOTES

5-3 Trusting God: A Battle for Child Access

One of the greatest joys of not judging others is becoming more capable of discerning God's will in a difficult situation. His will is hidden in a foggy, thick cloud that is made up of your messy judgments. Nowhere is the cloud of judgments foggier than in a major conflict. Whether it is World War II or an all-out divorce battle, conflict forces you to figure out what price you are prepared to pay to stand up for what you believe in. Often, you don't *know* what you believe in until you have the conflict!

I believe that most divorces happen because of a lack of respectful conflict. Couples drift into the forty foot zone of emotional distance, feeling unloved and resentful. Then when the separation or the affair arrive, years of pent up anger emerges. That anger blinds a person. They become focused on success, not purpose.

Surely there is no emotional pain that is greater than having the person to whom you have vulnerably revealed your every wart and weakness to utterly reject you, publicly attack you and then become your most bitter enemy. In an ugly divorce, the main goal is to make the other person *pay* for the suffering you are feeling. If he or she wants to see the kids, don't let him or her see the kids! If your ex-doesn't want to see the kids, then pressure him or her to take the kids more often. If he wants to settle for x dollars, ask for $x + 20\%$. If he is willing to accept that, then ask for another 20% on top of that! I once had a female friend of mine read a letter I was intending to send to my ex-wife during our separation. My letter began, "I want…" My friend said to me, "Don't write 'I want.' Whatever you want is exactly what she won't give you!" It is little wonder that the horror of post-marriage atomic bombs are causing people to get married later in life, live common law or not enter a committed love relationship at all!

When your future relationship with your children, your lifelong savings, and your future earnings all hang in the balance, the worst side of normally sane people emerges. The hammer comes out in full force, with no mercy. The more money a couple has, the more they are able to fund the boomerang self-destruction of taking legal action.

When you focus on being non-judgmental, you are shifting your heart out of the blame-and-condemnation gear and into neutral with your engine still running. Then you will hear the Lord's voice—His will for you in a difficult situation. When you discern His will, you will know it. His will may not be logical.

His will may scare the daylights out of you. But there will be no doubt as to what's important now for you to do.

When I was still a seeker, God proved his presence to me beyond a shadow of a doubt. His proof appeared like He does so many times in the Bible—in the midst of a great battle! In my case, the battle was with my ex-wife. At one point, we had spent one and a half years in an acrimonious, legalistic battle over child access. Her goal was to give me as little access time as possible. My goal was to get as much access time as I could get, up to 50% of my son's time. One of the sources of my rage during that time was the realization that the legal system is stacked against fathers. Unless my ex-wife voluntarily agreed to give me shared custody (decision-making rights that are separate from child access rights), at least in our legal jurisdiction, then the courts would automatically grant her sole custody. She established this from day one by refusing to have contact with me, except through her lawyer. My lawyer advised that I had no chance of overcoming this strategy unless I could prove she was an alcoholic or drug user, of which she was neither. I was toast. After long months of overcoming my judgmental anger over this injustice, I came to the peaceful realization that what was important for me was access time, not decision-making rights.

Settling a divorce means overcoming the ultimate game of being judgmental. Either person can make the experience as long and drawn out as he or she wants, continually shifting the goal posts whenever a settlement appears imminent, just to keep the war going. Vengeance is the goal at this level of being judgmental! Each move further justifies a new and even more punitive counter-attack. After sixteen months, I was tiring of the battle. We had been to court four times, spent $50,000 each in legal fees and were looking at our third thirty-seven page legal separation agreement. She was ready to sign it. All I had to do was sign and I was done with the agony.

I looked over the agreement. In simple terms, I was to get about 16% of my infant son's time in the form of two evenings a week and one overnight every other weekend, scaling up modestly as he approached the age of five. The longest no-access period was five days, from Wednesday evening before her weekend to Monday evening after her weekend. I decided to ask her for a one hour visit at lunch time on Fridays, to break up the five day period. I thought this was reasonable as she was at work and our son was with a nanny. *"This should be a no-brainer,"* I thought. To my shock, she flatly refused. "Trust me," she responded.

"Once we stop fighting, then I'm sure I will feel better about giving you more time."

Her track record during our separation gave me no confidence whatsoever in that answer. I snorted in disgust and was left to deal with my awful dilemma. Do I sign the deal and trust her to give me that hour later? The weight of my son's entire life weighed heavily on me. Did he deserve more than a visiting uncle for a dad? My only other option was to tear up the deal and begin a prolonged sole custody battle, which my lawyer had clearly outlined for me: two more years, another $100,000 in legal fees, and a full-blown trial that would include dragging family and friends onto to the witness stand. What a brutal pair of choices!

Still, something deeper did not feel right about this deal. I had a strong sense—call it intuition, gut-feel, quiet inner voice—telling me not to sign this deal. The thought of not signing brought quivers to my knees. I had had enough. I was tired and fed up. Still, I could *not* shake the feeling. Finally, I took the issue to the men's therapy group I was attending at the time. To my surprise, they were totally supportive of why I might be better off to engage this further battle, though they could see why I would rather not.

Though I was not yet a believer, in my heart I felt God was speaking to me in a loud, clear voice. After vacillating for over a week, I took a leap of blind faith and decided to trust Him. I sent back the unsigned agreement and advised I would be beginning a new round of formal legal proceedings. Her lawyer expressed their shock and disgust at my decision. However, I noticed they never came back to offer me the one hour I had requested! I took her to court three more times in the following three months. Then a judge sat both of us down to advise us about the nasty realities of a full-blown trial. I could see that she was hearing this news for the first time, while I was already at peace with it. I was ready to spend every last dime I owned on this.

These are the moments where each of us must search our heart and soul to be honest with ourselves. Many times, my judgmental, self-righteous anger about the unfairness of the legal system against men had me emotionally swearing that I would fight to the death to change the system. However, every time things settled down, I noticed this urge would go away, confirming that this was not my real purpose, but just emotional steam. This time I felt different. I felt great conviction that I was doing God's will both for me and for the good of my son's relationship with me, without any desire for vengeance towards her, even if she perceived it that way. I also felt aware of the possibility that God wanted my ex-wife to face this experience for His own reasons.

After the judge's talk, to my surprise, she made a move. Her lawyer called. They were ready to negotiate a final settlement, requesting a full day, four-way negotiation between the two of us and our two lawyers. I readily agreed. We spent nine exhausting hours in a downtown office tower, haggling out every detail. By late that day, we had a signed agreement. I received exactly *double* the amount of access that I would have had over the previous agreement that I had refused to sign.

I went home and cried. Instead of elation, I felt humbled, crushed like a bug. There was not a shadow of doubt in my mind that I had done *nothing* to earn this gift. God laid this gift on me freely and completely. All I did was obey His will, in spite of my logical mind and in spite of my fears. The enormity of His gift highlighted how deeply God loves me, in spite of my sinful, unworthy nature. It took me nearly three weeks to come out of this deep suffering, one that was similar to mourning—a mourning of joy. He must have had a purpose for me because one month later, I gave Him my life at an altar call at a local Christian festival. I was on fire with the Holy Spirit that very night, a fire that glows more fervently every time I let go and trust God to lead the way.

Group Study: Purposeful Lesson 5-3: Reconsider a conflict in your life. Explore a new range of possible solutions. What if you gave in completely—what do you fear would happen? What if you did the opposite and took a strong stand—what would that look like? Remember the Steady Hands symbol. What is your space to defend? What is his or her space for you to support? Are you trying to "teach" the person a lesson or punish them in any way for how they have hurt you? Do your motives reflect the love of Jesus in your heart?

NOTES

5-4 Money vs. God: You are More Than a Will

Few subjects trigger our judgments more deeply than money. Friendships, business partnerships and marriages rip apart when money matters are not satisfactorily resolved. One wealthy divorced couple I know of have spent more than eight years battling over the division of their assets, using one legal maneuver after another to maintain a soul-destroying drubbing of each other. I met a sixty year old woman in a divorce support group who spoke about the financial impact of her lost thirty year marriage. She cried over the loss of her dream for a comfortable retirement. She spoke bitterly of how she supported his career for thirty years, only to see the rewards of retirement go to another woman. It turned out that her divorce happened eight years earlier. Holding on to her judgments about her ex-husband had seemingly become her purpose in life.

Money affects us deeply—our standard of living, our acceptance in the community and our self-image as successful or as failures. The mere fact that we tend to carefully hide our financial truth from others is evidence of how fearful we are of being judged about our financial situation. However, money itself is non-judgmental. It is completely neutral. Our debts are our debts. The amount is the amount. Our investments are a number on a sheet of paper. How we feel and what we choose to do about theses numbers is an entirely different matter! Paul writes, "For the love of money is the root of all evils, and some people in their desire for it have strayed from the faith and have pierced themselves with many pains." (1 TI 6:10 NAB)

Money is power. A lot of money gives a person a sense of security, along with status and influence. Not enough money triggers our deepest fears of inadequacy, failure and dying on the street in poverty. A Christian financial planner I know phrased it beautifully for me when he said, "We say, 'In God we trust.' In truth, it is "In Money we trust."' To live a purposeful life means examining the power we give to money to make us feel approved and disapproved. We must examine our beliefs that money is the measure of our success. Many Christians equate money with being "blessed." But Jesus speaks of our challenge around money many times. He taught, "'You cannot serve both God and Money.' The Pharisees, who loved money, heard all this and were sneering at Jesus. He said to them, "You are the ones who justify yourselves in the eyes of men, but God knows your hearts. What is highly valued among men is detestable in God's sight." (LK 16:13-15 NIV)

Many of us believe that because we do not desire great wealth, that we are right with God about money. We just want our daily bread, plus a trip to Florida once a year! However, it is only when the very foundation of our financial footing is under attack that we begin to see how much we rely on money for our peace, and not God.

The Lord has blessed me with the experience of having a lot of money and then no longer having that money. When I was thirty-eight, I was wealthy by some people's standards. I was making a lot of money—more than $250,000 a year. My wife earned a similar income, making us a very well-off couple of D.I.N.K.'s—Double Income, No Kids. Our $400,000 house was mortgage-free. We had liquid savings of over $200,000 on top of tax-sheltered investments of $300,000. While not fabulously wealthy, I certainly felt that I could buy anything I really wanted without a second thought.

Making a lot of money does a funny thing to you. You start thinking about *why* you're doing what you're doing. What's the *point*? Is it just to make more money? "Will more money make me happier?" I asked myself. "How *much* more will make me happier?" I wondered. I decided to calculate the answer. Little did I expect that running a small spreadsheet of numbers would change my life forever.

I have always been a numbers guy, so I loved doing this. I decided to calculate how much money we would need to retire comfortably, and how quickly we could acquire that money. I made up a *fifty* year spreadsheet—covering the possibility that I might live well into my eighties. I worked out how much we needed to save per year, applied compound interest assumptions to our assets, made an inflation assumption to account for rising prices over fifty years, and crunched out various scenarios in both tax-sheltered and unsheltered investments.

The sheet was a mass of little black numbers in tiny boxes. I could readily change my assumptions and instantly see the impact of different scenarios on how much money we saved, how soon we saved it, and how long it lasted—depending on when we retired, how much we spent every year of retirement, and how fast inflation ate up our buying power. The answer itself was nothing any decent financial planner couldn't tell you. I figured we could retire by age fifty-four and we would comfortably survive financially until we were ninety.

The effect of the exercise on my heart was an entirely different matter. I began to ask myself, is this all there is? Will I work at this frenzied pace for the next fifteen to twenty years, only to retire to a winter condo in Florida and a summer cottage in northern Ontario for the next thirty years thereafter? Even worse, will a fat bank account be all that I have to show for my efforts? That was my great fear—a vision of living to seventy years of age with a tombstone that said,

John Kuypers
1957–2037
"He made money"

That vision shocked me. I realized that my heavy focus on retirement planning at my tender age was telling me just how unhappy I was about the work I was doing. I was wishing my life away, believing that my happiness lay twenty years ahead in the bliss of retirement! What a trap I had fallen into, I thought grimly.

I also wanted to leave more than a will behind. At that time, I wanted my life to have meaning so that when I left this world, the world would in some way have known that I was here. I guess I wanted to leave behind a legacy. I had been given the great joy of having five separate, challenging, and rewarding careers. I had lived the "good life," traveling to exotic places like Monte Carlo, Hawaii, Switzerland, Greece and the Caribbean. I had even actively pursued buying a multi-million dollar business, believing that pursuing my "entrepreneurial" dreams would satisfy my insatiable thirst to accomplish something meaningful in life. None of these had satisfied me.

Sometimes God gets you by giving you everything you ever wanted. That's when you know for sure that there is nothing in this world that can fill the emptiness inside you. God put that financial analysis in front of me and it was a clanging wake up call! I had the frightening opportunity to see the future—my very own future, just like Ebenezer Scrooge in Charles Dickens' classic tale, *A Christmas Carol*. Each column of numbers stared at me—another year, another series of mind-numbing, repetitive consulting contracts, business deals and client schmoozing. Fifteen of them in a row, maybe twenty if things didn't go perfectly well. Then came thirty years of golf, beaches, social events and shopping to "fix up the place," wherever and whatever that might evolve into. My stomach heaved. God was at work. That was ten years ago, before I was born again. Now I have a new dream:

If I touch but one life,
change but one moment,
I will have done Thy will.

If that person should be
someone dear to me,
so much the better.

And if it is my wife
for whom I give my life
I will die with glee.

Son or daughter,
mother or father,
Am I more than a will?

And if I call myself,
saved by the Christ
If I leave not love behind,
I have not lived at all.

An honorable sentiment, you might say. Then comes the doing part. Do you have to go broke to love God and love your neighbor? Do you have to be penniless? Before I became a believer, one major reason I resisted God was my fear that He would lead me to a poor and penniless life. Isn't that the image we have of saints? We see true Christians who live in destitute places under impoverished conditions. I think of Mother Teresa as an example.

A few months after my spiritual conversion, the Lord used the shocking death of a lifelong friend to steer me in an entirely new direction. I gave up my consulting business and began a new calling to write my first book. I had nearly $300,000 in savings. I figured that amount would last me five years. Five years is a long time. I thought, *How could it ever take me five years?*

Five years went by. In the sixth year, my savings plummeted down to $16,000, all used up to live on while I continued to be true to what I believe is God's purpose for my life. That was when my anxiety skyrocketed. My bragging rights on having taken my blood pressure down from 120/80 to 90/64 disappeared. I was back up around 118/60. My peace was shaky. My ability to stay fully present waned, notably my ability to remember things almost effortlessly. My anxiety rose while my income hovered around $15,000 a year, well below the $60,000 a year I needed to bring in for our lifestyle. Our financial situation frightened my wife tremendously and contributed significantly to her leaving me the second time.

The absence of money is a severe test of your faith in God. The Lord blessed me with this test. The first lesson I learned was that the peace I had felt in the previous four years, since my time of being born again, had been rooted in money. I didn't believe that until my money was actually gone. Then I knew it to be true. This was a most humbling moment. I had to admit to myself that my seemingly unshakable sense of peace and feeling present was anchored in *money*! "Oh God! Increase my faith!" I prayed, just as Jesus' disciples did when he taught them they must forgive seventy times seven times.

I pray regularly for His peace, focusing on my awareness that I am always safe in the present moment. We have a roof over our head, clothes on our back and food on our table. God faithfully provided me with the means to write my first book and to start a new career speaking and doing workshops on this topic. I remain aware that at any time my family and I are four months or less away from having to sell our house in order to pay our bills. Nevertheless, He has never failed to faithfully provide the money we need.

Deciding to lead a purposeful life comes at the risk of not being successful in a worldly sense. Financial and career failure can lead to devastating self-judgment. When the stock market crashed in 1929, people jumped out of windows in despair. Men in particular are almost hard-wired to correlate their sense of self-worth with their career and financial success. The fear that friends and colleagues will suddenly treat a man who is a financial failure as a leper is deep and real. The pressure from wife and kids who don't want to be impacted by a man's drop in income can be very severe. Fellow Christians shake their heads and quote this passage from St. Paul, "If anyone does not provide for his immediate family, he has denied the faith and is worse than an unbeliever." (1 TIMOTHY 5:8 NIV) This passage is often used to justify an all-consuming focus on career, or to judgmentally label some men as "deadbeat dads." The real challenge is, are you doing God's will as some men as "deadbeat dads." The real challenge is, are you doing God's will as you earn your living? Jesus said, "Not everyone who says to me, 'Lord, Lord,' will enter the kingdom of heaven, but only he who does the will of my Father who is in heaven." (MT 7:21 NIV) As believers, we must reconcile the dilemma of serving God ahead of money, while providing for our families to the level that God blesses us with, not to the level our family and friends would prefer from us.

The life of Jesus and his apostles shows us that doing the will of God is a risky way to live, both for ourselves and for our loved ones. Can we possibly deny that the women in Jesus' life abhorred his purpose? That his mother Mary would have wanted to see him hang on a cross? That Mary Magdelene, Martha and his apostles wanted to lose this magnificent man of love from their midst? What would have happened to the black civil rights movement in the United States if Martin Luther King had taken the attitude that his wife and family's comfort must come ahead of his purpose in life? Jesus clarifies this for us: "Brother will hand over brother to death, and the father his child; children will rise up against parents and have them put to death. You will be hated by all because of my name, but whoever endures to the end will be saved." (MT 10:21-22 NAB)

Few of us are asked to take a stand for Jesus that means giving up our lives, or being cruelly rejected, abandoned and attacked. Nonetheless, this is an understandable fear of every believing Christian. Every faith-driven person faces the same difficult challenge: how to be true to your purpose and risk not being "successful" in the eyes of those around you.

Group Study: Purposeful Lesson 5-4: What are some difficult choices that you face between God and Money? Explore these scenarios to stretch your mind:

- If you gave away 50% of your net worth, who would you give it to and why? How would you feel about the resulting impact on your lifestyle?
- You decide to stop working right now and live off your savings. What would you do with your new-found time? How would your loved ones react?
- Discuss how you and your spouse manage your day to day finances. Do you share one bank account? How do you resolve differences in how you decide to spend money?
- You decide to reveal publicly how much you make and how much you are financially worth. What judgments might come your way?

NOTES

_____

_____

_____

_____

_____

5-5 Building Trust: Judgments among Christians

There are few experiences in life that I treasure more than being in the presence of someone whom I fully trust. I know I can be who I am and not feel afraid of whether the person will approve of what I say, feel or do. The real me is safe with him or her, and I can relax and feel at peace. This person is loving me the way Jesus loves me— without judgment. He or she has no agenda and no needs. I can count on one hand the few people with whom I have truly felt this level of peace. I myself struggle to give this kind of experience to the people who cross my path. I still have too many needs. I still have something to prove and something to lose. I still want to be successful in their eyes.

As a generalized group, the people I feel most unsafe with are other Christians. I feel a much keener sense of approval and disapproval among Christians than I do among non-Christians. Many others have shared a similar sentiment with me, so I know that I am not alone. The purpose of this study section is to consider the ways in which we, as Christians, each in our own way, are judgmental toward one another, and to consider setting our disapproval aside for the greater cause of standing out in the world on account of our love for our fellow man as committed members of the Body of Christ.

Once you become a Christian, there are many things about which to feel judgmental. Like the Sadducees and Pharisees, we have a rule book called the Bible. It is our fallen nature to want to be like God, and God's own rule book is an irresistible foundation upon which to approve and disapprove of those around us. When my wife left me for the second time and then returned, the one person in our lives who was most critical and judgmental of her decision was a Christian. This person refused to speak to either of us for several months, primarily because I as a Christian had failed in this person's eyes. My wife's non-Christian friends and family, on the other hand, immediately respected and supported her unexpected change of heart.

There is a television evangelist whom I respect and admire, and whose name I won't mention, who further highlights the phenomenon of the "judgmental" Christian. He was making the point that we must follow the inerrant Word of God as written in the Bible. He pointed out how Catholics don't do this. Then he pointed out how liberal Protestants also fail to do this. Finally, he assured his audience that conservative Christian churches like his strictly follow the literal words in the Bible. I have no doubt that his intentions were honorable in exhorting us to be true to God's word. Nonetheless, the message that some Christians are more righteous than others was plain to see. His hypocrisy was immediately evident as I saw women in his church who had uncovered heads, in contravention to Paul's teaching, **"But any woman who prays or prophesies with her head unveiled brings shame upon her head, for it is one and the same thing as if she had had her head shaved."** (1 COR 11:5 NAB)

We are saved by grace and not by works. Therefore, why do we focus on creating distinctions of superiority and inferiority based on works? This is what Jesus said to the apostle John about differences in how people speak out in His name: **"Master, we saw someone casting out demons in your name and we tried to prevent him because he does not follow in our company."** Jesus said to him, **"Do not prevent him, for whoever is not against you is for you."** (LK 9:49-50 NAB)

The extra-judgmental nature of many Christians works against the very purpose for which Jesus came to earth—to save the whole world. Instead, we see the body of the Christian church fighting against itself in numerous ways. Individual churches break apart, adamant that one group is more right than another. Groups align to oust an unwanted pastor or to refute one doctrinal teaching over another. Entire countries fight civil wars, as we see in Northern Ireland among Catholics and Protestants. As Christians, we seem to want to commune with people who believe *exactly* what we believe. Our tolerance is low and the love we radiate is also low. We are succeeding in building new churches but failing to grow the church body. We are failing because we are too judgmental of one another.

I am no exception. I was raised as a Roman Catholic. As I grew into my late teens, I grew very critical of my church. I felt the Mass was ritualistic and deathly boring. I judged our priest's sermons as monotone and irrelevant. I daydreamed my way through church every Sunday. I hardly knew a soul in the whole church, even after eight years of attending that particular parish. The moment I moved out of my parents' house at the age of eighteen, I immediately stopped going to church. I returned only when I felt terribly down and lonely—about once or twice a year. God still had a string on me, much as I wanted to declare myself independent of Him!

Some twenty years later, while I was a still a seeker, I went "church shopping." I felt determined to have an open mind and consider all the possibilities. Nonetheless, I felt some fear and trepidation about entering a non-Catholic church. An old memory flooded back to my mind. When I was nine years old, I innocently attended a vacation bible school at the local Baptist church with a neighborhood chum for one summer morning. When my mother found out, she was aghast! "We are Catholic," she admonished me. "We are not allowed to go into other churches!" I wanted to ask why, but I didn't dare. I just felt sad that I couldn't go back and paint more pottery with my friend. Eventually, I came to peace about the shortcomings of the Catholic Church, appreciating its strengths as the church of my heritage. As my friend Bruce who first evangelized me said, "You have to separate your relationship with Jesus from the religious institutions of this world. Remember, they're all run by sinners, too!" His words of wisdom were what first softened my heart to begin reading the Bible.

Nonetheless, churches can be a scary place. Either you are warmly greeted, or coldly ignored. Warm greetings are scary because you wonder if they are going to pressure you to join right away? What if you enter and don't know how to do things the way they do things? Perhaps you won't know the words to their prayers and songs and everybody will notice! Being ignored is scary too. Sure, it's nice to enter as if you're invisible. At least that way, you don't feel eyes on you, checking out how you look and wondering where you're from, why you don't have a husband or wife with you and whether you're a real believer. Once you get a sense of how the place operates, however, then you wonder why people don't introduce themselves to you! This is just another example of the crazy dilemma of Near and Far. This must drive pastors and lay ministers over the edge, trying to overcome the fearful nature of people.

Pastors can also feel like scary people. One time, a pastor read my first book, *What's Important Now*. Later, he greeted me with a warm smile and said, "John, we have to talk. You have got some things wrong, my friend!" I could feel a shiver run down my spine. I knew him to know the Bible practically by heart, cover to cover, with a mind like a steel trap. Oh, how we dislike having someone point out how we've missed the mark! I don't know how a pastor overcomes the intimidating image of the fire and brimstone preacher who sees all of our faults and casts judgment upon us for messing up. Of course, most pastors are the opposite, being kind and supportive in nature. Then you wonder what they're really thinking. Are they just being nice, not real?

One of the most profound ways in which to build trust and let our light shine as Christians is contained in what I believe are **the ten hardest words to live up to in the Bible**; "Simply let your 'Yes' be 'Yes' and your 'No,' 'No.'" (MT 5:37 NIV) This teaching is difficult because we agree to do things too readily. We *support* when we should *resist*. This habit is anchored in our desire to win the approval of others by making promises we later regret.

I have often been guilty of this. I lightly say, "Sure, I'll give you a call …" and never get around to it. I agree to take on a volunteer role, and then back out of it as the time approaches because something else more important came up, often related to work, a.k.a. money! My wife sometimes asks me to finish up a load of laundry she started before heading out to her job. I agree to do it and then get absorbed in my own busy day. When she comes home, she asks, "Did you do the laundry?" I feel a flush of embarrassment wash over me. "Oh no! I completely forgot!" I say apologetically. One time she responded, "I guess I just won't ask again." I don't blame her. I have invited her judgment of me by my failure to let my Yes be Yes.

However, I encourage anyone on the receiving end of this kind of failure to be Wise, not Smart. You can decide your loved one is a lost cause or you can nudge him or her an inch forward. When you give the person a bottomless cup of chances to perform, you give yourself the chance to encourage any forward movement he or she might happen to miraculously exhibit! Each of us has the opportunity to lift our loved ones if we can first be non-judgmental about their failings.

Another common version of the challenge of living up to your word is *avoidance*. I am surprised at how often I notice that Christians avoid the risk of being real by simply avoiding the person. We don't return phone calls. We listen to a request and politely avoid giving the person a straight answer so we don't "hurt" their feelings. We look the person in the eye and say we'll do something but then don't. Then we often avoid the possibility of being rebuked by simply avoiding our brother or sister all together. Do we really think they'll forget? All of us have failed in this area, and the only solution that I know of is to humbly and frankly own it, seek forgiveness and offer to make up for it if we can. Humble admission of one's own failings is the greatest benefit of being non-judgmental. Otherwise, your pride and shame will hold you back, leaving behind a trail of bumps and bruises in your relationships.

Even if you live up to Jesus' demanding teaching in this area, others won't. Then you will be like the frog in this story:

There was a scorpion who wanted to cross the creek. Seeing a frog, he asked the frog, "Will you let me climb on your back and carry me across the water?"

And the frog replied, "No, I will not."

"Why not?" asked the scorpion.

"Because you will sting me!" replied the frog indignantly.

"I promise that I won't," said the scorpion. So the frog agreed to carry the scorpion across the creek. As soon as they safely landed on the other side, the scorpion turned his tail and stung the frog. The frog gasped in pain and cried out, "But you said you wouldn't sting me! How could you?"

The scorpion replied, "I couldn't help myself. It's my nature."

We are sinners by nature. Our challenge is to set people free, to have compassion when they fail, to be real ourselves, to be wise about how we respond to others, and to keep our eye on our purpose—loving them as Jesus loves us.

Group Study: Purposeful Lesson 5-5. What more could you do to leave the "loveprints" of Jesus on those you love? If your loved ones could ask you for anything, what would they want? If you are not sure, what do you need to do to find out? If you do know, what would you have to do differently? Listen more?

Support their goals? Take a personal interest in their passions? What would that look like?

NOTES

_____

_____

_____

_____

_____

5-6 Give Without Expecting Anything Back: Parking Lot Hog

We learn at an early age that love is conditional. If you do what others expect, they will love you. If you don't, they won't. I felt quite a shock when I realized that I give in this way. I began to notice that this was a constant running pattern in my mind, especially at work. "What's in it for me?"—WIIFM for short. Everything was a trade-off—good contacts, a referral, money or expertise of some kind. Even as I wrote this book, I was aware from time to time that I wanted to sell enough copies to earn enough money to live on. When I felt discouraged that this might not happen, I could feel the strong pull to stop writing and focus on earning a business income.

To give without expecting anything back is a tall order. Yet in order to be purposeful, this is exactly what God wants from us. Jesus tells us, "So you also, when you have done everything you were told to do, should say, 'We are unworthy servants; we have only done our duty.'" (LK 17:10 NIV) Non-judgment is foundational to giving without a return because expecting a return is exactly what causes us to be judgmental! We give, and if we don't get back, we hold it against that person. A lifetime of experiences of this kind has heightened my sensitivity to being caught in this judgmental cycle.

My wife and I were once planning a vacation. She called an old friend who lived in the area we intended to travel, asking her for advice on accommodation and tourist activities. Her friend responded by inviting us to stay with them rather than renting accommodation. We were thrilled and gratefully accepted their generous offer.

After a long drive, we arrived at eight o'clock in the evening, having not yet eaten dinner. Our intention was to announce our arrival and then go out and get our own dinner. Our hosts immediately insisted on making us a spaghetti dinner. My wife accepted without hesitation, while I grew wary. An old judgmental trigger of mine was being tickled—if you accept a gift, you owe them. What scared me was the awareness that many people will offer you their generosity, but will expect something in return. My fear lay in the possibility that I might fail to figure out what their expectation was. My mind flitted immediately to what we could do to repay their hospitality. Perhaps take them out for dinner? Buy them a gift? Underneath my sociable self, I felt mildly anxious. As it was, an opportunity arose later in the evening. They suggested we have a barbeque the next night. We offered to buy the ingredients and prepare the meal, which they accepted with delight. My anxiety level instantly eased. This experience reminded me of just how deeply rooted this aspect of our judgmental nature is rooted in me.

When we accept a gift from others, we are in danger. We owe them. Their generosity is conditional. If we don't repay them properly, they may judge us. A little voice echoes in the back of our head, hearing them gossiping with disapproval to mutual friends. We imagine them saying things that we heard them say to us about others! "We invited them over for dinner three times but they've never invited us over for dinner even once!" "I helped the guy get that job interview and now he won't even meet with me for lunch!" We carry our judgments around like debits and credits in our bank account, tracking our gifts to others and believing that either of us can cash in at any time.

I have a friend whose generosity always touches me. He is quick to pay and often arrives with gifts for our children. However, he is reluctant to accept the favor in return. I surmise that he is protecting himself against the danger of being in my debt. To be in debt to someone is to invite being judged if you fail to repay, and to expose yourself to being pressured to doing something you don't want to do. We see this stereotype in movies like *The Godfather*, where Marlon Brando does the dirty work for others, while they in turn are in his debt. He accumulates great power over others in this way, and is willing to use violence to enforce his power. His conscience rests easy while murdering those who are not "loyal" because they failed to pay their debt to him.

My parents were conditional givers. Their intentions were highly honorable. They wanted to teach me that nothing in life is free and that I must earn my way. My allowance was based on doing daily chores on our family farm. If I wanted them to drive me to an event, they would often slip a condition in such as, "If you hoe the garden, I will drive you to your ball game." They also used the reverse approach. "You didn't help clean out the barn, so now we won't let you go to that party." I remember deciding at an early age that I did not want to ask my parents for much, because there would be a price to pay that I was not going to like! This didn't stop me from asking, of course. Instead, this dynamic set us up for many judgmental experiences. I developed the bad habit of doing the bare minimum in order to get what I wanted, while judgmentally grumbling that they were "making me do it."

My first marriage was heavily immersed in this method of controlling each other. "I gave in on this, so now you owe me. You have to now give me what I want." We created beliefs about what was "fair," and we then used these to leverage each other to get what we wanted. For many men, even sex can feel like a type of bargaining tool. Our wives "give" us sex as if it is for our exclusive pleasure at their expense. We know this to be true when she says, "Again? You just got lucky the other day!" Of course, that statement can make for a good laugh if delivered in a non-judgmental, loving way. The real intention is conveyed in the underlying attitude and tone-of-voice, not the words.

When you are non-judgmental, you become courageous and bold, just as the disciples were. They communicated their love for Christ in their everyday words and deeds. Their boldness was heightened because they were no longer afraid of being judged by other people. When you embrace Jesus' teaching to not judge, your confidence soars because you know in your very soul that you will not strike out judgmentally towards others, even if they become highly judgmental and threatening toward you. On that basis, it is much easier to be real, not nice, in a way that leaves others feeling loved and lifted, not criticized and made to feel small.

Opportunities to touch others with the love of Christ that dwells within you arise on a daily basis. These are the moments of truth where you reach out to someone to intentionally leave a "loveprint" on them. Such a moment happened to me one Sunday morning after church.

Our church is large, with four thousand families registered and about that many individuals who attend the four services every week. While the parking lot is large, the exit lane is not. It is typically a five minute crawl to patiently exit out of the two lanes that lead to either a left hand or right hand turn onto the residential street.

From time to time, someone decides to park in the right hand lane of the only exit route, cutting the traffic flow in half and doubling the time to exit the lot. Often, this person has the good manners to hustle out and be among the first to leave. One particular Sunday, this was not the case. About ten minutes into our slow, arduous, car-by-car squeeze around this parked car, its owner appeared. Obviously in good spirits, he stood behind his car and chatted merrily with another group of people for another two or three more minutes.

I could feel the familiar niggle. "Accept or act?" I thought. "I don't want to accept," I concluded. "Yet neither do I want to act unkindly or harshly to this person. I want to *influence* him, not bully him. How can I do this?" I continued. "Just be straightforward," I said to myself. "Be real. Cut to the chase. Do it non-judgmentally and trust in the Lord after that."

By happenstance, my turn to pass by him and his car arrived just as he was about to step out from behind the car and seek to open his car door. He smiled broadly at me and generously waved at me to move past him before he attempted to get to the driver's door. I stopped my car and rolled down my passenger window, letting the cold winter breeze rush in on my young son sitting in the front seat.

"I'm wondering, my friend, if you would mind not parking in this place in the future?" I sounded pretty confident, I thought encouragingly.

He smiled back and said, "I wouldn't mind at all."

"Thank you. I really appreciate that. Have a great day."

"Thanks—you too!" We smiled at each other and drove on.

Being purposeful in a non-judgmental way is so powerful. This is when you are being real, not nice—without casting judgment on another. It is a great feeling to impact another person in a way that allows him or her to feel your conviction in a loving way. These are the moments when you are skating along the edge of another person's boundaries. I had no authority to "demand" that he stop parking in that most inconvenient place. Nonetheless, I certainly had plenty of material to work with to be judgmental. His parking in the laneway, combined with taking several minutes to appear, and then to take a further lackadaisical three minutes to chit-chat, provided ample material.

If you feel judgmental in situations like this, it will most assuredly appear in your tone of voice, even if you can hide it in your choice of words. You need to first get non-judgmental and present-moment focused. My favorite approach to doing this is to take a moment to "reframe" the situation. Suppose there had been absolutely no other parking spot available? Suppose our pastor had accosted him after the service and delayed him? Suppose the people he chatted with behind his car were unexpected old friends? Could I see how I might have done exactly what he did, given those possible scenarios? I have learned from long experience not to assume anything. Every assumption is based on the past and is therefore, as the mutual fund companies like to say, "no guarantee of the future." Further-more, I had to let go of my past experiences. If he had been the first person to ever park there, I would instantly have been more forgiving. Being non-judg-mental is much harder when you are aware that this is the umpteenth person to "rudely" park in that way. Focusing on the present-moment, without thoughts of past injustices, is crucial to breaking this automatic judgmental habit.

The biggest payoff of intentionally seeking to be non-judgmental in situations like this is that you become purposeful. You are wanting to touch the other person out of love, and not selfish gain. You become willing to risk that the other person will get mad at you for speaking up. This risk is so much easier when you are coming from a non-judgmental place. He is free to park there. Your purpose is to let your light shine on him. Your loving frame of mind will weave into your every thought, word, tone of voice and body language. You will communicate, "I love you", even as you are making an assertive request. You are being salt *and* you are loving your neighbor, both at the same time. At a minimum, I like to believe that I helped my brother avoid the fate of many judgments in the future from possibly hundreds of politely silent (doormat) but unhappy (judgmental) fellow parishioners.

If the purpose of life is to love God and love our neighbor, then we must use our gifts to do more than be merely non-judgmentally neutral towards our fellow man. We must reach into the lives of those we care about, letting them feel our love by the weight of our character, our generosity, and our willingness to humbly serve their needs, even at the expense of our own. The reward is love— the love and grace of the Holy Spirit and the peace of Christ which will permeate your entire being. Then you will be able to live as if you have nothing to hide, nothing to prove and nothing to lose. With nothing holding you back, you will enjoy everything that matters—God's eternal love.

Group Study: Purposeful Lesson 5-6. What are the ways in which you find it diffi-cult to freely give or receive? One common example is the difficulty of giving and receiving compliments. Try this exercise. In pairs, have one person compliment the other person's physical appearance, offering a flood of examples from clothing to hair to body. Have the other person receive those compliments by mirroring back what the first person said as each compliment is delivered. For example:

Person A: You have beautiful brown eyes!

Person B: You think I have beautiful brown eyes!

Notice and discuss any judgmental feelings that arise in each of you. What beliefs are you holding about people who give compliments?

NOTES

Afterword

A WORD OF ENCOURAGEMENT

In order to live in Christ, we must die to ourselves. When you embrace non-judgment in your relationship with your wife or husband, part of what must die is your dream that he or she is the creator of your joy. My wife and I call this "shattered dreams." This is the painful and humbling suffering aspect of being non-judgmental. They are free to be who they are, and you are intentionally accepting the resulting impact on you. For this reason, *Lesson One: You Set Them Free* is the most difficult lesson to learn.

My hope and prayer for you is that *Lessons Two, Three, Four* and *Five* will encourage you. When you allow yourself to be Real, you set yourself free from the shackles of reacting to the approval and disapproval of others. When you give Compassion, you discover that 90% of what used to bother you has nothing to do with you! When you focus on being Wise, you learn specific skills that help you get what you want from the people you care about, ending the cycle of despair that "she'll never change," or "he'll never do it my way." When you live with love as your Purpose in life, what's important now in your life shifts profoundly.

Touching another person with the love of Jesus that dwells within you becomes what's important. You will begin to notice the very real and profound truth that the only time to love someone is in the present moment. Your "in-the-moment" reaction will reflect love or fear. Love will become your instant reaction when you give up the delusion that you are nice, righteous, smart and successful. These values are the old you—your old self-image that was anchored in feeding your ego. You've given up your sinful delusion that you are somebody special who deserves certain things out of life.

Jesus did not get anything special in his earthly life. He came to serve, not to be served. For this, God has exalted him to the highest place. Your challenge in your relationship with your wife, husband, son, daughter, father or mother is to do the same. You must make loving them as they are, your highest goal. If you are withholding your love, guarding and protecting your heart from being hurt, you are missing the central point of Jesus' teaching and Jesus' gift to us on the cross. To love is to be vulnerable. We can only be fully vulnerable when we know we are loved by the One who matters.

As a married Christian, your vow, "Till death do us part," can feel like a prison sentence, living without joy, without love and without hope. In relationships of this nature, the feeling that you would rather die or *are* dying is not uncommon. With divorce rates as high as 50% in the Western world, society has given couples permission to divorce as the easy way out. However, God has not. His instruction has not changed. Your purpose is to learn how to love your wife or husband, not abandon her or him. Jesus is your role model, your teacher and your Savior—not only in eternity but also now.

I encourage you not to wait until your marriage is in a deep hole. I believe that the seeds of divorce take root within the first five years of a marriage. After that, the roots grow deep and the will to repair the damage grows weaker and weaker. However, it is never too late to learn how to love your husband or wife, father or mother, sister or brother, son or daughter, ex-wife or ex-husband. Get committed to learning how to love as a *calling*, not as a leftover hobby. If you feel ashamed of admitting you have something to learn about love, Satan has already won. I encourage you to not let money, embarrassment or "I'm too busy," handcuff you from openly seeking help from the many professionals and programs that are available to any man or woman who has the courage to seek, to ask and to act. Be prepared to commit to an on-going period of personal renewal, including small groups, journaling, therapy, coaching, books and courses.

May you know His deep and abiding peace, filled with faith, hope and trust that the loved ones in your life are of God's choosing, designed to teach you perfectly how to cherish them by leaning on God alone as your source of love. I pray this in Jesus' precious name. Amen.

ACKNOWLEDGEMENTS

These loving, generous people reached out and touched this book so that you, the reader, could have the most rewarding experience possible. Their wise thoughts, frank feedback and encouragement were the visible spirit of God for me as I wrote this book. Any mistakes or errors are entirely mine, of course. May God bless each of you!

Pastor Arie Van Eek
Jean Davies
Bob Cameron
Rick Tyler
Pastor Paul De Graaf
Mike Martin
Naomi Gold, editor

I offer a special prayer in gratitude to my wife Joanne who has courageously walked with me on my journey of faith. I also thank my children, family and friends who exposed themselves to my watchful eye, looking for and etching onto paper our collective stories of success and heartache. You are God's gift to me! May you feel my love for you, every day of my life.

—John Kuypers
August, 2004

Appendix

NINE STEPS FOR BEHAVIOR CHANGE

The WIN Leadership Goal-Setting Template™ will help you clarify what specific behavior bothers you about a person so you can develop a specific action plan to helpfully and intentionally influence them to grow.

1.	**Target Person:** (Who do you want to influence?)
2.	**What is your purpose in wanting to help this person?** (e.g. perform better, feel more joy, face tough issues etc.)
3.	**What is their current behavior?** (Describe what they do that you want to alter?)
4.	**What is the cost of "no change"?** (risks like hurting themselves, financial loss, spiritual losses, stress, engraining bad habits)
5.	**What is specifically happening?** (How often are they doing it, to whom, where, when, what brings it on?)
6.	**Leadership Goal** (Pinpoint the exact behavior you want them to Stop, Start or Keep doing. Break it down into one inch bite-size chunks. For example, cleaning up after dinner involves many steps including dish removal, dishwasher filling, counter & table wiping, putting leftovers in containers, and so on.)
7.	**Past Approach** (What have you tried up until now?)
8.	**Is it working?** (Has the person responded to your efforts to influence their behavior?)
9.	**What else can you do?** (See Lesson 4-3 for ideas. Be creative. Accept that this requires time and effort. They will feel your love, even if you botch up, if there is no disapproval in your heart and your intention is to be helpful.)

ABOUT THE AUTHOR

John Kuypers is the son of Dutch farmers who emigrated to Ontario, Canada in the 1950s. The second of five children, John's early life was profoundly influenced by the heavy demands on his family from his severely mentally handicapped older brother, who passed away into the Lord's loving hands in 2003.

John was a corporate vice president and a management consultant in sales, marketing and organizational change for nearly twenty years. Through the outreach of loving friends and the grace of the Holy Spirit, John became a born again believer in August, 1998, after a difficult two year divorce battle. John has since devoted his life to writing and teaching about personal leadership through being non-judgmental and present-moment focused. His first book, *What's Important Now*, was published for the secular market in 2002.

John is the founder of Steady Hands Men's Coaching Ministry, devoted to teaching Christian men relationship skills that prevent divorce and release couples from the prison of relationship despair. Through WIN Leadership, John also speaks, coaches and trains business leadership skills that build trust and influence without using traditional command and control leadership methods.

John lives with his wife Joanne and their blended family of four young children near Burlington, Ontario, Canada, where he is an active member in a vibrant local Roman Catholic church.

CONTACT US

To order copies of *The Non-Judgmental Christian: Five Lessons That Will Revolutionize Your Relationships,* please contact us at:

Present Living & Learning, Inc.
P.O. Box 40601
Burlington, ON
Canada L7P 3N0

Place book orders via the internet at **www.presentliving.com** Significant quantity discounts are available on multiple books.

E-mail John Kuypers at john@presentliving.com John appreciates hearing from his readers and will do his best to personally respond to every inquiry, letter and prayer of encouragement.

Stay in touch with us. Sign up for the Steady Hands monthly e-bulletin, offering readers around the globe moving, personal stories of relationships success stories and John's speaking and events schedule. Go to **www.steadyhands.org** and confidentially enter your e-mail address.

Enjoy John's first book, *What's Important Now: Shedding the Past So You Can Live in the Present* ISBN #0968968406. Go to **www.presentliving.com** to order.

Here is one typical testimonial about this book:

"If you have not read John's book, *What's Important Now,* then you are missing out. I was blown away with this book and it actually helped me change my perspective on achieving goals in life and evaluating what really matters. This book can change your life!"

— **Tony DeLiberato,**
CEO, Netrix, Inc.

WIN Leadership Executive Coaching & Training applies the core leadership principles from *The Non-Judgmental Christian* to the workplace.

WIN Leadership helps leaders improve performance by building trust and influencing people to excel, freely and willingly. Research shows that 80% of a person's job satisfaction is directly driven by the quality of their relationship with their immediate boss.

Managers learn to build trust in 30 seconds, 30 minutes, and 30 days+. Through workshops and one-on-one coaching, leaders rapidly acquire new skills to master the most difficult aspect of running an organization—managing people for results.

Please visit our website at: **www.winleadership.com**

STEADY HANDS

Men's Coaching
Ministry

The Steady Hands Men's Coaching Ministry is dedicated to preventing divorce and broken relationships among Christians. Up to 50% of marriages end in divorce, even among committed Christians. The devastation emotionally, spiritually and financially is incalculable. Quality of life crumbles and scars last a lifetime on spouses, children and every member of the extended family. We believe that there is a cure for divorce.

Through Jesus' teaching, "Do not judge," we give a Christian man hope and skills to intentionally and respectfully help he and his wife find joy in their marriage, shape his children's behavior and confidence, and help his most precious assets—his loved ones—feel the love of the Holy Spirit dwelling within him.

We coach Christian men to apply the five lessons from The Non-Judgmental Christian. Taking action is the key to success. We offer private one-on-one personal coaching, weekly men's groups, the Steady Hands Men's Coaching Course and introductory workshops and keynote speeches. Please visit our website at www.steadyhands.org for more information and to contact us.

Steady Hands is committed to transforming the relationship skills of Christian men. If you want to support us or join our divorce prevention ministry, contact us at www.steadyhands.org